This is an authorized facsimile
printed by microfilm/xerography on acid-free paper
in 1986 by
UNIVERSITY MICROFILMS INTERNATIONAL
Ann Arbor, Michigan, U.S.A.

WITHDRAWN

Wisdom, Christology, and Law in Matthew's Gospel

Wisdom, Christology, and Law

Harvard University Press

in Matthew's Gospel | M. Jack Suggs

Cambridge, Massachusetts 1970

For Chester Crow and Elmer Henson

ΔΟΥΛΟΙ ΑΓΑΘΟΙ ΚΑΙ ΠΙΣΤΟΙ

Preface

During the academic year 1963–64, I was engaged in the investigation of the relation between wisdom and apocalyptic speculation in Judaism under grants from the American Council of Learned Societies and the American Association of Theological Schools. The present study is a by-product of that year. The possibility of Matthew's use of the figure of Wisdom in the development of his Christology became a preoccupation of mine during the final, hectic days of packing and preparing to leave Heidelberg for Fort Worth. And the ill wind which accompanied us from Le Havre to New York provided me so much time in the cabin that this book was virtually in outline when we landed.

Yet, by the time we were again settled into the routine at home, a major restudy of program was under way in the seminary, so that finding time to pursue the project became a problem. It was the invitation to deliver the 1966 Spring Lectures at Lexington Theological Seminary which finally provided the special pressure which brought these notes together in a somewhat different form. An expanded version of the lectures was awarded a prize by the Christian Research Foundation, Inc., that year. In this way, my debt to institutions (not least, of course, to Texas Christian University) has grown—as has my appreciation.

The generosity of the academic community continues to surprise me. By correspondence and conversation, I have been aided on specific and general points by a host of colleagues. I would like to express my special gratitude to Kenneth W. Clark, Eldon J. Epp, Dieter Georgi, Helmut Koester, James M. Robinson, Morton Smith, Krister Stendahl, R. McL. Wilson, and James Dunkly. Their counsel on specific points has been quite valuable, but it is obvious that they must not share the burden of my errors.

Mrs. Bill Valentine and Mrs. Gene Johnson were patient and careful typists. The staff at Harvard Press was always understanding and helpful—the kind of people an author hopes will handle his book.

In addition, I would like to thank my family, who will remember the period of enforced silence in the automobile, as we sped down the Autobahn, while my wife took the dictation of the first notes which set this study under way; there have been other periods of such silence since and no doubt there will be again.

Except in a few places where a private translation was necessary, the Revised Standard Version of the Old Testament, Apocrypha, and New Testament has been followed. Quotations from the Pseudepigrapha have been taken from the edition of R. H. Charles.

M. Jack Suggs
Brite Divinity School
Texas Christian University
Fort Worth, Texas

Contents

Wisdom, Christology, and Law in Matthew's Gospel

Prologue

I had thought to subtitle this essay "A Footnote to Matthean Christology." The description would be wholly appropriate on several grounds:

(1) The study examines a quite limited number of synoptic pericopes which have been influenced by Jewish and early Christian speculation about Sophia. It is not claimed that this examination exhausts the material relevant to the subject in Matthew's Gospel, but a genuine effort has been made to explore the implications of the key pericopes.

(2) No attempt has been made to relate these Wisdom passages to all other facets of Matthean theology in a systematic manner, although the process of exegesis has required tentative probing of their significance for some other elements in the evangelist's thought (such as, for example, the Son of man).

(3) The investigation arrests the story of one of the most exciting currents in early Christian history (the speculation

1

about Sophia) at a particular moment in its development. We are concerned primarily with one frame in a moving picture; frequent flashbacks show the background of early Christian Wisdom thought in pre-Christian Judaism, but only occasional fugitive glimpses of Sophia's significance for later orthodoxy and heterodoxy appear. The frame selected for viewing is, however, of critical importance, for it illustrates the flux in first-century Christian theology which makes attempts at defining a simple apostolic orthodoxy premature. At the same time, I hope it will be clear that Matthew's contribution to subsequent developments is of considerable significance.

Yet, a subtitle which is appropriate on so many grounds is rendered impossible by one consideration. For too long, the traces of Wisdom speculation present in Matthew have been treated as tangential or eccentric traditions foreign to the purpose and theology of the evangelist. They constitute, in my opinion, certain proof that one aspect of Matthew's thought has been unfortunately neglected. The description, "A Footnote to Matthean Christology," cannot be used, because it is the express aim of this report to lift the Wisdom motif out of the footnotes of scholarly discussion, where it can be too quickly written off as an unexplained outburst of Johannine ideology. If the study succeeds in this modest objective, then the writer's purpose will be achieved.

I. Traces of a Wisdom Speculation in Q

This study proceeds from the assumption of the existence of the document commonly referred to as Q. That assumption has been vigorously assailed in recent years, notably by Austin M. Farrer (who regards it as dispensable) and William R. Farmer (whose objections to Q are a part of a larger assault on the conventional solution to the synoptic problem, as represented by B. H. Streeter's *The Four Gospels*).[1] Farmer's book has especially exposed the cumulative weaknesses of Streeter's argument for the priority of Mark. Yet, it does not appear to me that a viable alternative has been offered, and I am persuaded that the most serviceable hypothesis remains something like the generally accepted one—with the understanding that when we speak of "Mark"

---

1. Austin M. Farrer, "On Dispensing with Q," in *Studies in the Gospels: Essays in Memory of R. H. Lightfoot*, ed. D. E. Nineham (Oxford: Basil Blackwell, 1955), pp. 55, 86; William R. Farmer, *The Synoptic Problem* (New York: Macmillan, 1964); B. H. Streeter, *The Four Gospels* (London: Macmillan, 1925).

as a source of the other synoptics we have in view a document sufficiently distinct from our second Gospel as to be perhaps a different edition of it.

Literary Form of Q

The issue of Q, always treated cautiously in the accepted solution because of its hypothetical character, is another matter. The result of recent discovery and investigation—for me—has been to extend the plausibility of the Q hypothesis. In contrast to Farrer, I find it indispensable. The chief problem with Q has not been the relation between Matthew and Luke in the double tradition—that is, in their common material. The agreement between these gospels is so strong that some literary connection between the two must be postulated, and, on the whole, the evidence appears to favor their mutual dependence upon an outside source rather than direct dependence of one upon the other.

Until recently two serious objections to this solution made a firm decision in favor of Q somewhat difficult. The first problem· was an absence of any clear parallel to such a document, comprised almost wholly of sayings, in early Christian literature. Even the Didache, which obviously bears some kinship to the genre, could not provide by itself determinative support because of its special character. The second problem, which was no doubt intensified by the idea of a normative primitive kerygma (a first-century orthodoxy) derived from Paul and Acts, was the absence from Q of any real concern with the passion. This silence was even more difficult to understand in view of the fact that Q obviously has Christological[2] and eschatological[3] interests.

The first of these problems was met in part by the discovery at Nag Hammadi of a similar literary product, the Gospel of Thomas. A Coptic sayings-source related to previously known Greek fragments (Oxyrhynchus Papyri 1,

2. See Paul Feine and Johannes Behm, *Introduction to the New Testament*, rev. W. G. Kümmel, tr. A. J. Mattill (Nashville and New York: Abingdon, 1965), p. 56 (hereafter cited as Kümmel, *Introduction*); H. E. Tödt, *The Son of Man in the Synoptic Tradition*, tr. D. M. Barton (Philadelphia: Westminster, 1965), *passim*.

3. See W. D. Davies, *The Setting of the Sermon on the Mount* (Cambridge, England: Cambridge University Press, 1964), pp. 380–386.

654, 655), the Gospel of Thomas preserves some material contained in the canonical Gospels and other traditions independent of them. It satisfies in part the need for an example of a Jesus literature with minimal narrative content.

Yet, it must be admitted that the discovery of the Gospel of Thomas alone would not fully answer our need. Even with its evidence in, one could still argue as W. G. Kümmel did:

But now whether or not a very old tradition parallel to the synoptic tradition lies at the base of the Gospel of Thomas, the writing as such is doubtless no late form of the same literary category as Q, but a different, later stage of development in the tradition of Jesus' sayings . . . This conclusion follows not only from the lack of any narrative and any subject arrangement, but above all from the lack of any Christology and therefore any connection with the gospel development which emerged first in Mark. The Gospel of Thomas presupposes the meaning of Jesus' person in the role of Gnostic revealer, and thereby shows itself as a literary form of a later time.[4]

Although Kümmel's argument perhaps exaggerates the degree of "narrative and subject arrangement" in Q, implies an unacceptable idea of the uniformity of early Christian proclamation in its reference to Mark, and completely begs the question of the Christology implicit in Q, one cannot deny that the argument has considerable force on the surface.

However, the discovery of the Gospel of Thomas was more important than had been recognized at the time of Kümmel's thirteenth edition of 1963. The 1965 edition carries a supplement of footnotes, including a reference at just this paragraph to a highly significant essay by James M. Robinson.[5]

---

4. Kümmel, *Introduction*, p. 58.

5. James M. Robinson, "*ΛΟΓΟΙ ΣΟΦΩΝ:* Zur Gattung der Spruchquelle Q," in *Zeit und Geschichte: Dankesgabe an Rudolf Bultmann zum 80. Geburtstag*, ed. E. Dinkler (Tübingen: J. C. B. Mohr [Paul Siebeck], 1964), pp. 77–96 (hereafter cited as "Logoi"). Robinson's own translation and expansion of this essay will appear in H. H. Koester and J. M. Robinson, *Trajectories Through Early Christianity* (working title, Fortress Press). A draft of the enlarged essay was generously supplied by Robinson as this book went to press and has been used to clarify my understanding of one point about which I had been unclear as to the intention of the German version. I have made no systematic attempt to accommodate my translations to the language of the draft.

The effect of Robinson's study was to reverse Kümmel's judgment that "the Gospel of Thomas can teach us nothing concerning the origin and literary character of Q."[6] Robinson was able to show that Thomas and Q represent particular moments in the development of a literary *Gattung* with a history in Judaism and in "orthodox" and "heterodox" Christianity. In his view, the Gospel of Thomas stands at a transition point in the evolution of the *Gattung*. Ahead of it lies the full development of the "hidden sayings" requiring appended secret interpretation—with a document such as the Pistis Sophia at the end of the line. The evolutionary movement of the form ends in Gnosticism, but it also has "a prehistory which lies within the great Church."[7] Robinson makes his way behind the Apostolic Fathers and the synoptic Gospels to earlier collections of sayings similar to Q. He then proceeds to demonstrate that the real origin of the *Gattung* is to be sought in the wisdom collections of the Old Testament and Judaism, collections frequently identified in superscriptions or within the body of the texts as "sayings of this or that individual sage" or more generally as λόγοι σοφῶν, "sayings of the sages." He cites as a particularly noteworthy example of the genre the Pharisaic tractate Pirke Aboth and finally derives the technical term which he applies to the *Gattung* from the incipits which stand above several of the collections in the book of Proverbs.[8] He is able to demonstrate that Matthew shows a special awareness of the significance of the *Gattung*.[9]

Thus, not only the discovery of another "sayings document" in the Gospel of Thomas, but also Robinson's analysis of the *Gattung*, has effectively eliminated any reason for doubting the existence of Q *on the grounds of its literary uniqueness*.

Robinson's essay suggests the solution to our second problem, as well: that is, whether the primitive tradition could produce a document in which the passion played so insignificant a role as in Q. The *Gattung* in question exists precisely

6. Kümmel, *Introduction*, p. 58.
7. Robinson, "Logoi," p. 84.
8. "Logoi," pp. 94–95.
9. "Logoi," pp. 85–86.

as a vehicle for transmitting the words of the "sages." "That [this] suggests an understanding of Jesus as a σοφός," writes Robinson, "is established through the fate of the Jesus-tradition, as it alone makes this development completely intelligible."[10] He hints that the relation between Jesus and Sophia, the hypostatized Wisdom of Jewish speculation, is already tending in Q in the direction of understanding Jesus in precisely the role that Kümmel saw for him in the Gospel of Thomas, the role of the Gnostic revealer.

All of this is to say that, not the absence, but the presence of a passion *narrative* would be an occasion for surprise. This is true, not because Q is fully Gnostic and those who valued it would necessarily have no interest in the crucifixion,[11] but because the nature of the *Gattung* itself puts the emphasis in another place, namely, on Jesus as the dispenser of a wisdom which is indispensable to life. The *Gattung* has to do, not with the reporting of redemptive occurrence, but with the transmission of revealed truth.

It is more significant that the collected sayings contain no references to the crucifixion as redemptive event. It is at least strange that in Q we must reckon not only with the absence of a passion story, but also with an indifference to its redemptive significance so complete that the passion kerygma has had no effect on the sayings.

It is in some such sense that Robinson can speak of the "development of the hypostatized Sophia into the Gnostic redeemer" as bringing "the tendency at work in the *Gattung*" to its conclusion.[12] Nevertheless, we must be very careful not to import the conclusion of the tendency into every manifestation of the genre. It is only necessary to point again to the Pirke Aboth to remind ourselves that the *Gattung* does not *of itself* require the gnosticising development. Indeed, if Matthew's Sermon on the Mount were abstracted from its position in the Gospel, it would serve as an admirable

10. "Logoi," p. 96.

11. Not all Gnostics, however, may be assumed to have had no interest in the crucifixion, as the Gospel of Truth makes particularly clear (e.g., Gospel of Truth 18:19–29, 20:25–34).

12. "Logoi," p. 96.

example of the genre.[13] The fact that Matthew has incorporated Q in a gospel, which is characterized by historical concern and reaches its climax in the passion and resurrection, imposes significant limitations on the gnosticising potentiality of the *Gattung*. At the same time, Matthew's interest in Jesus as a teacher and his arranging sayings material as discourses (particularly the Sermon on the Mount) show the influence of the form on him and his allegiance to it. As we shall see, Matthew's problem with Q stemmed from the fact that in his community the document was being interpreted in a gnosticising[14] fashion,[15] not from his distrust of the form as such.

Thus, while the statement is doubtless correct that the *Gattung* "Sayings of the Sages" possesses an incipient tendency in the direction of Gnosticism, how Q is to be interpreted depends on considerations in addition to that of literary type. The Gospel of Thomas itself indicates the ambiguity of the *Gattung* as evidence of theological bias. It is true that the Gospel of Thomas was found along with other items with a markedly Gnostic content, a fact that has enhanced our estimate of its own Gnostic character; it is only by knowing in advance that we have to do with a work popular in Gnostic circles that we are led to derive a Gnostic meaning

13. So William R. Farmer in conversation; Farmer's remark was made in a discussion in which he indicated that the question of sayings collections in the early church is independent of particular source theories and that, in his judgment, the hypothesis that both Matthew and Luke used Q for the "double tradition" is not required to prove the existence of such collections. *Cf.* Robinson, "Logoi," pp. 85–86.

14. By "gnosticising" I always mean "moving in the direction of Gnosticism, not yet fully Gnostic." It does not seem to me wise to speak of the raw materials out of which second-century Gnosticism emerged as Gnostic; that term should be reserved for the more radically dualistic, more highly mythologized thought forms of the later period. I suppose that I might have chosen the adjective "pre-Gnostic" rather than the word "gnosticising" in conformity to the Messina Colloquium "Proposal." I have elected to retain the term "gnosticising" because it seems better to convey the dynamic, interactive character of the phenomena being examined here. See Ugo Bianchi, ed., *The Origins of Gnosticism: Colloquium of Messina, 13–18 April 1966* (Leiden: E. J. Brill, 1967), pp. xx–xxxii; *cf.* R. McL. Wilson, *Gnosis and the New Testament* (Oxford: Basil Blackwell, 1968), *passim* and esp. p. 58.

15. Although Luke's doctrine of the Spirit appears to owe something, perhaps a great deal, to the figure of Wisdom, I can see no clear signs that the third evangelist was aware of the problems with which Matthew was concerned in his treatment of Q. This may mean only that Q was interpreted differently in his community. On the other hand, it may be a product of Luke's unusual insensitivity to or lack of information about some currents in the life of the church.

10

from many of its sayings (some of which are not theologically tendentious at all).[16] Moreover, documents of any genre might be capable of a Gnostic or gnosticising interpretation. Marcion, if he was a Gnostic, found an abbreviated version of Luke to his liking. According to the usual opinion, Cerinthus used Mark.[17] To this day the Fourth Gospel is, with good reason, well-supplied with "Gnostic interpreters." That is to say, the gospel form is no guarantee against Gnostic interpretation and the *Gattung* "Sayings of the Sages" does not require it.[18] Still, the "Sayings" literature unquestionably has a potential for Gnostic usefulness, as Robinson has shown on the basis of Gnostic literary remains. On the other hand, while Gnostics might *interpret* canonical gospels, the Gnostic documents which bear the title "gospel" usually have little in common with the genre of the synoptics and John.

A Gnosticising Interpretation of Q?

Two questions about Q are raised by the foregoing discussion: (1) Was Q *susceptible* of a Gnostic or gnosticising interpretation? (2) Did Q *invite* interpretation of this kind?

The first of these questions must be answered before we can proceed further. The second should be given a provisional answer in the present chapter, but must be treated more fully as we proceed with the examination of the Gospel of Matthew.

The answer to the first question has been provided, again by James M. Robinson, in an article which appeared in 1962.[19] Following a discussion of U. Wilckens's theory of a

---

16. *Cf.* Hans Jonas, *The Gnostic Religion*, 2nd ed. rev. (Boston: Beacon, 1963), pp. 308–309.

17. But see Davies, *The Setting of the Sermon on the Mount*, p. 194.

18. Helmut H. Koester (in private correspondence) properly emphasizes that there is a clear distinction to be made between "internal developments of a literary genre on the one hand, and interpretation of existing literature on the other." Koester's understanding of the *Gattung* under discussion and particularly of its theological tendency is set forth in "One Jesus and Four Gospels," *Harvard Theological Review*, 61 (1968), 203–247, esp. 211–230. In his view, Q was already a "secondary version" of a primitive sayings source into which "the Son of Man was introduced to check the gnosticizing tendencies" of the source (p. 230).

19. James M. Robinson, "Basic Shifts in German Theology," *Interpretation*, 16 (January 1962), 76–97 (hereafter cited as "Basic Shifts").

developed Sophia myth in Corinth, he proposes to read Q as it might have been understood by a "person whose thinking was oriented . . . in terms of the first part of 'The Hypostasis of the Archons' from Nag Hammadi."[20] If one makes the terms Sophia, Spirit, and Word refer to the same entity, it would thus be possible to read Q in a radically Gnostic fashion.

The "Word of God" comes upon John the Baptist (Luke 3:2), whose teaching is presented. Then the "Spirit" descends upon Jesus (Luke 3:22), whereupon his teaching is presented (Sermon on the Plain or Mount). Then John and Jesus' relation to each other and their mutual rejection is discussed (Luke 7:18–33), ending with the vindication of Sophia.[21]

Robinson's exposition of Q along these lines is carried through briefly but thoroughly and clearly demonstrates the possibility of reading it through Gnostic spectacles; thus read, it is a report of the activity of the heavenly Sophia in her envoys, John and Jesus.

The obvious problem with this exposition is that Robinson has chosen very late eyes through which to view Q, so that one appears to be asked to assume that Q might have been read as a document of second-century Gnosticism in the middle of the first century. In fact, in private correspondence Robinson indicates that the "Hypostasis" was chosen for illustration of a trend and that "clearly Q itself is far from that advanced." The choice of "The Hypostasis of the Archons" as the vantage point from which to examine Q is, for that reason, unfortunate. Most of what Robinson has to say could have been said against the background of Jewish wisdom

20. "Basic Shifts," p. 82; see also Ulrich Wilckens, *Weisheit und Torheit*, Beiträge zur historischen Theologie 26 (Tübingen: J. C. B. Mohr [Paul Siebeck], 1959); for a critique of Wilckens's theory, see H. Koester's review in *Gnomon*, 33 (September 1961), 590–595.

21. Robinson, "Basic Shifts," p. 83. Robinson apparently defines Q so as to include Luke 3:2, 22, which verses, as Krister Stendahl (in private correspondence) notes, may not belong to Q. However, Robinson's exposition does not demand this definition. Q does begin with the message of the Baptist and it does proceed with the preaching of Jesus; this is brought together in a passage which discusses the relation of Jesus and John, concluding with the statement, "Wisdom is justified by her children (works)" (Luke 7:35, Matt. 11:19).

speculation. That is, the relevant background for understanding Q is not fully developed Gnosticism with its highly
articulated Sophia myth, but the gnosticising Judaism which
is to be found in such writings as the Wisdom of Solomon. In
the last analysis, however, Q belongs at some point on the
line of development which extends from the Wisdom of
Solomon (for example) to second-century Gnosticism. It is
capable of being read as the report of Sophia's action in her
envoys.

Wisdom's Oracle of Doom

Having said so much, we have really moved beyond the
question whether Q *can* be interpreted in the light of a gnosticising Wisdom speculation; there appear to be solid indica-
tions that Q invited such interpretation. That can only be
stated here as a hypothesis. However, we can now begin in a
preliminary fashion to examine the hypothesis by turning
our attention to Luke 11:49–51 and its parallel in Matthew
23:34–36.

The Oracle's History

Behind the Matthean and Lucan forms of this passage,
two prior stages in the history of the paragraph can probably
be discerned. It certainly was preserved in Q, which probably
took the logion from a Jewish *Vorlage*. While many of the
considerations which make such a history plausible for our
passage will become clear only in the course of the ensuing
exposition, it will be well to introduce certain literary considerations here in a preliminary fashion. The saying occurs
in Matthew and Luke in the following forms:

Matt. 23:34–36	Luke 11:49–51
(34) [διὰ τοῦτο] ἰδοὺ ἐγὼ [ἀποστέλλω] πρὸς ὑμᾶς [προφήτας] καὶ σοφοὺς καὶ γραμματεῖς· [ἐξ αὐτῶν ἀποκτενεῖτε] καὶ σταυρώσετε, καὶ ἐξ αὐτῶν μαστιγώσετε ἐν ταῖς συναγωγαῖς ὑμῶν [καὶ	(49) [διὰ τοῦτο] καὶ ἡ σοφία τοῦ θεοῦ εἶπεν· [ἀποστελῶ] εἰς αὐτοὺς [προφήτας] καὶ ἀποστόλους, καὶ [ἐξ αὐτῶν ἀποκτενοῦσιν] [καὶ

13

διώξετε] ἀπὸ πόλεως εἰς
πόλιν·
(35) ὅπως ἔλθῃ ἐφ' ὑμᾶς
πᾶν [αἷμα] δίκαιον
[ἐκχυννόμενον] ἐπὶ τῆς γῆς

[ἀπὸ] τοῦ [αἵματος Ἄβελ]
τοῦ δικαίου [ἕως] τοῦ
[αἵματος Ζαχαρίου]
υἱοῦ Βαραχίου, ὃν ἐφονεύσατε
[μεταξὺ] τοῦ ναοῦ [καὶ τοῦ
θυσιαστηρίου.] (36) ἀμὴν
[λέγω ὑμῖν,] ἥξει ταῦτα
πάντα ἐπὶ [τὴν γενεὰν
ταύτην.]

διώξουσιν,]

(50) ἵνα ἐκζητηθῇ
τὸ [αἷμα] πάντων τῶν
προφητῶν τὸ [ἐκκεχυμένον]
ἀπὸ καταβολῆς κόσμου ἀπὸ
τῆς γενεᾶς ταύτης,
(51) [ἀπὸ αἵματος Ἄβελ]
[ἕως
αἵματος Ζαχαρίου]
τοῦ ἀπολομένου
[μεταξὺ τοῦ θυσιαστηρίου
καὶ] τοῦ οἴκου· ναὶ
[λέγω ὑμῖν,] ἐκζητηθήσεται
ἀπὸ [τῆς γενεᾶς
ταύτης.]

The bracketed words require a literary relation between Matthew and Luke—which is to be explained by their mutual dependence on Q. As the contexts in Matthew (23: 29–33) and Luke (11:47–48) show, in Q the saying followed the "woe against the builders of the prophets' tombs." This means that in Q it was found in a setting dominated by direct address. The absence of direct address in Luke 11:49–51a is hardly to be explained unless third-person speech was present in Luke's source; Matthew appears to have altered the saying to conform to the pattern of direct address in 23:29–33, 36.

According to Luke 11:49 the saying is to be attributed to the Wisdom of God, but according to Matt. 23:34 it belongs to Jesus himself. Luke's form is surely that of Q: Luke would hardly change an I-saying into a saying of the "Wisdom of God," especially since it is clear from Luke 7:29–30, 35 that the third evangelist has no interest in speculation about Sophia (as will be seen in Chapter Two).

If it is indeed the Wisdom of God who speaks, then she speaks before the rise of history; this means that Luke's future tense (11:49, ἀποστελῶ) rather than Matthew's present (23:34, ἀποστέλλω) is from Q. Probably Luke's ἀποστόλους and perhaps Matthew's σοφοὺς καὶ γραμματεῖς have been added by the evangelists. In Matt. 23:34 14 the words καὶ σταυρώσετε have certainly been added by the evangelist; Luke could hardly have omitted them if they had been present in Q. Also, in Matt. 23:34 καὶ ἐξ αὐτῶν μαστιγώσετε ἐν ταῖς συναγωγαῖς ὑμῶν and ἀπὸ πόλεως εἰς πόλιν carry obvious Matthean tones and in part recall Matt. 10:17 (of the Gospels, it is only in Matthew that μαστιγόω appears in contexts not limited to the scourging of Jesus). In Matt. 23:35 πᾶν αἷμα δίκαιον must be the evangelist's; Luke's τὸ αἷμα πάντων τῶν προφητῶν (11:50) is demanded by Q's context. For what I trust are obvious reasons, I think that Matthew is responsible for ἐφ'ὑμᾶς, τοῦ δικαίου and υἱοῦ Βαραχίου in 23:35.

The remaining differences between Matthew and Luke do not appear important for the purpose at hand, and it is now possible to supply a hypothetical form of the saying which excludes the most significant elements contributed by the evangelists. I have rendered the passage in English to avoid giving the impression that I regard this hypothetical form as a word-for-word, rather than an approximate reproduction of Q. In my opinion, the reconstruction is accurate enough to make it possible to isolate traces of the saying's pre-Christian origin.[22]

Therefore also *the Wisdom of God said*, "I will send them prophets (and wise men and scribes?), and some of them they will kill and persecute, that the blood of all the prophets shed from the foundation of the world may be required of this generation, from the blood of Abel to the blood of *Zechariah*, who perished between the altar and the sanctuary. (Amen?) *I tell you*, it will be required of this generation.

There are three signs in the saying in this form which strongly suggest that Q has taken the saying over from an

22. The fact that Lucan expressions are usually translated means only that Luke's fidelity to the saying's original third-person style, future tenses, and quotation format, together with his avoidance of obvious Christian editorial changes like those in Matthew, makes his form closer to Q *in general*. Thus, in the passage for which Luke 11:50 and Matt. 23:35 offer the parallels, I have translated Luke's (probably editorial) ἵνα ἐκζητηθῇ rather than Matthew's ὅπως ἔλθῃ only because Matthew has more changes in this verse of a substantive character (ὑμᾶς, δίκαιον, τοῦ δικαίου, υἱοῦ βαραχίου). And, where the sense of the parallels are basically similar, it seemed better to work as much as possible from the Gospel which contained the words essential to Q's meaning (in this case, Luke's πάντων τῶν προφητῶν).

earlier source. These are indicated above by italics. The words "the Wisdom of God said" are best understood as a formula which introduces an oracle found in some previous work where it was attributed to Sophia. "Zechariah" is too remote a figure to be meaningful in a saying which *originated* in Christian circles. The switch to direct address in the last sentence ("I tell you") shows this sentence to be secondary.[23] The purpose of the added sentence in direct address is to apply a judgment pronounced by Wisdom to Q's generation. If this sentence is eliminated, the saying is left in a form which could have stood in a Jewish source—probably a lost wisdom apocalypse.

Form-critical analysis strengthens the case for such a history of the saying. It obviously belongs to the category of what would be called in the Old Testament an oracle of doom. Indeed, the fact that both Matthew and Luke report this saying in connection with preceeding "woes" would lead us to see here *in Q* an excellent example of the "speech of reproach" followed by an "oracle of doom" which is characteristic of the prophets. The form is described by Bentzen (the emphasis is his):

Speeches of reproach may . . . be introduced by the word "*Woe!*", otherwise the exordium of curses . . . The *oracle of doom* following the speech of reproach is generally introduced by a "therefore" (*lākēn*). But sometimes the order is inversed [sic.].[24]

It is possible that the Q setting for the doom oracle (in the "woes" against the scribes) was suggested by its context in the *Vorlage*. In that case, Is. 5:18–24 would provide a model to which the passage could be compared:

23. *Cf.* Ernst Haenchen, "Matthäus 23," *Zeitschrift für Theologie und Kirche*, 48 (1951), 55, reprinted in *Gott und Mensch, gesammelte Aufsätze* (Tübingen: J. C. B. Mohr [Paul Siebeck], 1965), pp. 29–54. E. Earle Ellis, "The Gospel of Luke," in *The Century Bible*, ed. H. H. Rowley and Matthew Black (London: Nelson, 1966), pp. 170–172, tries to trace the saying to "a Christian prophet or group of prophets." His argument relies heavily on phrases in Matt. 23:34 which must be editorial and on the term "apostles" in Luke 11:49 "even though the order is unusual."

24. Aage Bentzen, *Introduction to the Old Testament* (Copenhagen: G. E. C. Gads, 1948), 1: 199.

> *Woe* to those who draw iniquity with cords of falsehood . . .
> *Woe* to those who call evil good and good evil . . .
> *Woe* to those who are wise in their own eyes . . .
> *Woe* to those who are heroes at drinking wine . . .
> *Therefore,* as the tongue of flame devours the stubble,
> and as dry grass sinks down in the flame,
> so their root will be as rottenness
>   and their blossom go up like dust;
> for they have rejected the law of the Lord of hosts,
>   and have despised the word of the Holy One of Israel.

In a nearby passage (Is. 5:8–10) the prophet cries:

> *Woe* to those who join house to house,
>   who add field to field,
> until there is no more room,
>   and you are made to dwell alone
>   in the midst of the land.
> *The Lord of hosts has sworn in my hearing:*
> "Surely many houses shall be desolate,
>   large and beautiful houses without inhabitant . . ."

It cannot be determined whether the oracle of doom was connected with a speech of reproach in "woe"-style in the *Vorlage* followed by Q. There is, in any case, no question about the form of the saying under discussion (Luke 11:49–51, Matt. 23:34–36); it belongs to the category of the doom oracle.

Usually, such oracles in the Old Testament are attributed to Jahweh, and they are frequently accompanied by an implied or express, "Thus saith the Lord." For example, in the Isaiah passage last cited, the oracle is introduced by the formula "The Lord of hosts has sworn in my hearing." This suggests that the meaning given the phrase "Therefore also the Wisdom of God said" (Luke 11:49) should be in accord with what the form "oracle of doom" will permit. That is, the subject should be taken to be a person or personified entity of divine status. Several possible understandings of this phrase may be considered.

(1) It has already been suggested that the oracle was   17

originally a part of a pre-Christian Jewish writing. However, in both Matthew and Luke the saying is credited to Jesus. We must reckon with the possibility that the logion is a genuine saying of Jesus.

On this assumption, it might be asserted that Jesus here refers to himself as "the Wisdom of God" just as he elsewhere is said to call himself "Son of Man." However, the use of the aorist εἶπεν (Luke 11:49) virtually excludes the interpretation of this saying as a genuine word of Jesus with this meaning. We would expect instead "Therefore, the Wisdom of God λέγει" in agreement with the present forms in the context.

The aorist suggests that, if this saying was spoken by Jesus at all, he would be quoting Sophia and not referring to himself as God's Wisdom. Moreover, if Jesus considered himself to be the representative of Sophia, it is not clear that Jewish speculation about Wisdom provided the background in terms of which Jesus could have made this full identification of himself with Sophia intelligibly. In spite of what is sometimes said about the "incarnation" of Wisdom in her representatives in pre-Christian Judaism, it would be difficult (in fact, I think, quite impossible) to find a place where the distinction between Sophia and her envoy is obliterated in just this way.

It is, in my judgment, very unlikely that we are dealing here with a genuine saying of Jesus. If it is treated as genuine, then it must be regarded as his quotation from a lost Jewish source and assigned a meaning similar to that discussed under (5) below.

(2) A second interpretation would take the phrase "the wisdom of God" to mean something like "God in his wisdom."[25] I think it very likely in the light of Luke 7:29–35 that this is what *Luke* understood by the expression (see below, Chapter Two). However, this precise circumlocution is not found elsewhere, to my knowledge, and the interpreta-

---

25. T. W. Manson, "The Sayings of Jesus," in *The Mission and Message of Jesus* by H. D. A. Major, T. W. Manson, and C. J. Wright (New York: E. P. Dutton, 1938), p. 394; printed separately as *The Sayings of Jesus* (London: Student Christian Movement Press, 1949), p. 102.

tion ignores the role of Wisdom at other places in the Q tradition.

(3) It is convenient to introduce at this point in a brief fashion the question of the use of the phrase in Q. It might be claimed that Q has identified Jesus with Sophia and in this way has either attributed a Wisdom oracle to him or transformed a saying of Jesus into a saying of Wisdom.[26] Several considerations tell against this understanding. As in (1) above, the tenses used both in the introductory formula and in the remainder of the saying are, to say the least, clumsy if this was Q's intention. Matthew, who *does* give the oracle as a saying of Jesus, changes all the verbs to the present tense in order to give this sense. Q, however, leaves the oracle in a form that would be more easily understood as a quotation *by* Jesus than as a saying *of* Jesus. More important, as we shall see continually, Q probably thinks of Jesus as the last of Wisdom's messengers, not as incarnate Wisdom.

(4) It has been proposed that "The Wisdom of God" was the title of a lost Jewish apocalypse and/or wisdom writing, which is here quoted. In precisely this form, the proposal encounters difficulties that cannot be overcome with ease. In the first place, if the form-critical judgment that this is an oracle of doom is correct, then the oracle should have a personal subject rather than a literary one. In the second place, the introductory formula does not fit the usual pattern of formulas used for citation. As Manson observed, "so far as usage in the gospels is anything to go by (*cf.* Mt. 22 [24]; Mk. 7 [10], 12 [36]; John 1 [23], 12 [39–41]), [the Q formula] would imply that the wisdom of God wrote the supposed book, as Moses was believed to have written the Law, or David the Psalms, or Isaiah the book of Isaiah."[27]

(5) The most probable explanation is that the passage is quoted from a lost wisdom-apocalypse where it was given as an oracle of personified Wisdom.[28] Only this solution which

---

26. See Ulrich Wilckens, "σοφία, σοφός," *Theologisches Wörterbuch zum Neuen Testament*, ed. G. Kittel and G. Friedrich (Stuttgart: W. Kohlhammer, 1933–   ) 7: 516.

27. "The Sayings of Jesus," p. 394.

28. It might be possible to add another alternative, namely, that the oracle was a piece of oral tradition which had no literary history prior to its incorporation in Q.

is supported by Matthew's substitution of ἐγώ for ἡ σοφία τοῦ θεοῦ avoids the problems discussed above. It does not contradict the general pattern of citation formulas in the New Testament (4), avoids reliance on a hypothetical circumlocution (2), and refrains from a premature identification of Jesus with Sophia (1 and 3). Moreover, it accords with the form of the saying as an oracle of doom, for the ascription of doom oracles to Sophia is no new departure in the wisdom tradition. Already in Proverbs 1:

> Wisdom cries aloud in the street;
>   . . . at the entrance of the city gates she speaks:
> ". . . Because I have called and you refused to listen,
>   have stretched out my hand and no one has heeded,
> and you have all ignored my counsel
>   and would have none of my reproof,
> I also will laugh at your calamity;
>   I will mock when panic strikes you,
> when panic strikes you like a storm,
>   and your calamity comes like a whirlwind,
>   when distress and anguish come upon you.
> Then they will call upon me, but I will not answer;
>   they will seek me diligently but they will not find me.
> Because they hated knowledge
>   and did not choose fear of the Lord,
> would have none of my counsel,
>   and despised all my reproof,
> therefore they shall eat the fruit of their way
>   and be sated with their own devices" (verses 20a, 21b, 24–31).

It is thus possible to identify four stages in the transmission of the oracle we are investigating: (a) the lost Jewish wisdom-apocalypse, (b) Q, (c) Luke 11:49–51, and (d) Matt. 23: 34–36.

Because we do not possess the *Vorlage*, we are at the obvious

---

If this were true, I cannot see that it would make a great difference in our argument. However, it appears to me that the oracle's introduction by a formula employing an aorist verb is only explained if a document such as that proposed above is postulated.

disadvantage of having to interpret the oracle at the earliest stage without the assistance of such contextual hints as are provided in the three Christian sources. Yet, the identification of the passage as an oracle of doom spoken by Sophia permits us to set the saying in the broad context of the late Jewish wisdom tradition which provides the essential clues to its meaning. It is clear that the Wisdom of God speaks "before the beginning of the earth" (Prov. 8: 23)[29] and declares that she will send her messengers to men. The oracle employs the familiar theme that Sophia comes in her agents for the purpose of revealing the ways of righteousness and thus redeeming men. Wisdom of Solomon 7: 27 summarizes an old motif, "In every generation she passes into holy souls and makes them friends of God and prophets." The idea of Wisdom's repeated efforts among men through her envoys is elaborated in Wisd. of Sol. 10–11 into a new interpretation of *Heilsgeschichte*, in which Israel's history is seen as determined by Sophia's providential guidance of the people through chosen vessels in "each generation."

It is only a short step from the Wisdom of Solomon to the apocalyptic and fully deterministic view of history which is implied in our oracle. In the oracle of doom under consideration here, the "prophetic generations" are represented as reckoned in advance by Sophia—from Abel to Zechariah; the meaning obviously is "from the first rejected 'friend of God' to the latest."[30] Between these termini, we are expected to be able to interpolate the intervening generations. History is the story of the rejection and persecution of Wisdom's envoys (a subject about which we will be concerned later). The view of history is as frozen as that of the Apocalypse of Weeks (1 Enoch 93, 91: 12–17)—in which Enoch, "born the seventh in the first week" learns the whole course of the "weeks" from the heavenly tablets (93:2). From before creation, Wisdom knows the destiny of her prophets whose blood will be required of this γενεά.

---

29. See Haenchen, *Zeitschrift für Theologie und Kirche*, 48 (1951), 53, 55.

30. It is unfortunate that the oracle was not originally written in English, since then we could speak of all the prophets of Wisdom—from A(bel) to Z(echariah)! This is precisely the idea.

The fact that we cannot refer to the context of the lost apocalypse makes decisions about some specific points quite difficult. How, for example, was the expression "this γενεά" intended to be understood in the *Vorlage*? It is sometimes argued that γενεά should be translated "race."[31] The reasoning is that the translation "this generation" would be inappropriate to the conceived time of speaking—that is, to the precreation stance of Sophia. Plausible as this position is on the surface, one cannot be fully confident of its correctness. While it is logical that pre-existent Wisdom should not speak of the final generation as "this generation" (that is, as contemporary with Wisdom's speaking), we are too familiar with the inconsistency of apocalyptic literature in matters of this kind to make the absence of anachronism an absolute norm of interpretation. Moreover, the formula "this γενεά" meaning "this generation," which occurs frequently in the Synoptics in sentences which imply judgment (usually, condemnation) is not new, but is dependent on similar Old Testament formulations as in Gen. 6:1, 7:1; Num. 32:13; Deut. 32:5, 32:20; Ps. 94 (95):10; Jer. 7:29 (in all of which γενεά translates דור).[32] It is perhaps not important that we make a choice between two possible renderings at the first stage, for the immediate and broader context in the Christian documents makes it clear that Matthew, Luke, and Q intend "generation" to be understood.

A similar but more serious question concerns the titles given to Wisdom's envoys by the lost apocalypse (or, for that matter, by Q). According to Luke, they are called "prophets and apostles," while Matthew speaks of "prophets, wise men, and scribes." Luke's ἀποστόλους is usually regarded as a Christian alteration.[33] That judgment, although probably

---

31. See J. D. Schniewind, *Das Evangelium nach Matthäus: Das Neue Testament Deutsch*, ed. P. Althaus, 8th ed. (Göttingen, Vandenhoeck and Ruprecht, 1956) 2: 237; Haenchen, *Zeitschrift für Theologie und Kirche*, 48 (1951), 54–55.

32. *Cf.* Friedrich Büchsel, "γενεά," in *Theological Dictionary of the New Testament*, tr. G. W. Bromiley (Grand Rapids: Eerdmans, 1964–   ) 1: 663.

33. *Cf.* Haenchen, *Zeitschrift für Theologie und Kirche*, 48 (1951), 53; Rudolf Bultmann, *The History of the Synoptic Tradition*, tr. John Marsh (New York: Harper and Row, 1963), p. 114, n. 1; A. H. McNeile, *The Gospel According to St. Matthew* (London: Macmillan, 1938), p. 339.

correct, is not quite so obvious as is frequently assumed. What would ἀπόστολος (or, perhaps, its Aramaic equivalent) mean in a pre- or non-Christian writing?[34] If one were to translate it by a colorless synonym for "apostle" (like "messenger" or "envoy"), would the difficulty that we feel with the term not largely disappear? Moreover, the "lament over Jerusalem" (Matt. 23:37–39, Luke 13:34–35), which is also a Sophia saying and which in Matthew immediately follows the oracle of doom, bemoans the city's "killing the prophets and stoning τοὺς ἀπεσταλμένους to you." If both these Wisdom sayings are derived from the same *Vorlage* (which is not certain), there would be good reason to entertain the possibility that ἀπόστολος was a title for Wisdom's envoy in that source. Further, while Matthew's "wise men and scribes" *sounds* more Jewish to trained Christian ears than Luke's "apostles," there is evidence that "prophet" (Matt. 5:12) and "scribe" (Matt. 13:52) were ecclesiastical titles in Matthew's church—and far less evidence than one

---

34. Whether the primitive Christian apostolate was derived from the Jewish *shaliach* (cf. K. H. Rengstorf, "ἀπόστολος," in *Theological Dictionary of the New Testament*, 1:407–46) is, of course, not the issue here, since we are speaking of the possibility that the term appeared in Q's source. Recent studies of the apostolate in early Christianity tend to favor a pre-Christian understanding of ἀποστόλους in Luke 11:49. Walter Schmithals, *Das kirchliche Apostelamt* (Göttingen: Vandenhoeck and Ruprecht, 1961), p. 86, n. 7, thinks that—while the term may have been introduced by Luke with reference to Christian apostles—it is more likely that it is to be explained by the source of the oracle, which he designates a Jewish "*Weisheitsbuch.*" Hans von Campenhausen, "Der urchristliche Apostelbegriff," *Studia Theologica*, 1 (1947), 102, also speaks of an "unknown wisdom book;" concerning the use of ἀποστόλους in Luke 11:49, he writes: "es handelt sich um die 'Gesandten,' die Gott selbst im Laufe der Heilsgeschichte bis zuletzt in die Welt und zu seinem ungetreuen Volke geschickt hat; aber um die von Lukas sonst vorausgesetzten zwölf Apostel oder überhaupt um irgendwelche christliche Apostel im engeren, technischen Sinne handelt es sich offensichtlich nicht." Rengstorf, *Theological Dictionary of the New Testament*, 1:428, believes that at Luke 11:49 the term refers neither to Jesus' disciples nor to the twelve. Cf. Reinhart Hummel, *Die Auseinandersetzung zwischen Kirche und Judentum im Matthäusevangelium*, Beiträge zur evangelischen Theologie 33 (München: Chr. Kaiser, 1963), 27.

As the term does not appear again in the pericopes investigated in this study and has such an uncertain place in the history of this passage, speculation about the meaning of ἀπόστολος would be inappropriate in this essay. It may be noted in passing that our "prophets in each generation" have some characteristics in common with Schmithals's Gnostic apostles.

23

might anticipate that "apostle" was such a title.[35] On the other hand, the literature of ancient Judaism in passages influenced by the wisdom tradition provides good parallels for each of Matthew's titles: for example, Enoch is the "scribe of righteousness" (1 Enoch 12:3, 15:1); Daniel is clearly a wise man; and Sophia does send her prophets. On the whole, if we are to assume that either Matthew or Luke preserved the original wording, the wide Christian usage of ἀπόστολος probably is enough to tip the scales against Luke's reading. Yet, the fact that Matthew's "wise men and scribes" does serve his view of church offices leaves room for doubt. It is possible that the wisdom-apocalypse agreed at this point with neither Matthew nor Luke, but referred to Wisdom's representatives as "prophets" only.

It is now possible to summarize. Luke 11:49–51a and Matt. 23:34–35 record variant forms of a Q saying which was derived from a now-lost apocalypse. It is an oracle of doom spoken by the heavenly Sophia who prophesies that her prophets will be killed and pronounces judgment on "this γενεά."

The Oracle in Q

To this point, the oracle has been examined primarily as a piece of pre-Christian Jewish wisdom apocalyptic, with occasional references to its place in Christian materials. It is now necessary to turn to Q and ask about the meaning of the oracle to the tradition represented there.

The Lucan form of the saying, and its relation in both Matthew and Luke to preceding "woes," shows that Q intends it still to be understood as Wisdom's oracle of judg-

---

35. Ἀπόστολος appears only once in Matthew (10:2) in the sentence, "The names of the twelve apostles are . . ." Even here, the Sinaitic Syriac reads "twelve disciples," which von Campenhausen, *Studia Theologica*, 1 (1947), 104, n. 1, regards as original.

The prominence of scribes (and prophets) in the Matthean church is argued by R. Hummel, *Die Auseinandersetzung, passim*, especially pp. 17, 18 ("Es ist offensichtlich, dass der Begriff des Schriftgelehrten als Bezeichnung jüdischer Autoritäten zurücktritt, weil er in die Kirche des Matthäus Eingang gefunden hatte."), 26–38, 59–62. *Cf.* Georg Strecker, *Der Weg der Gerechtigkeit*, Forschungen zur Religion und Literatur des Alten und Neuen Testaments 82 (Göttingen: Vandenhoeck and Ruprecht, 1962), 37–39.

ment. The most significant modification of the saying at this stage is the addition of the sentence, "Yes, I tell you, it will be required of this generation" (Luke 11:51b, Matt. 23:36). The adoption of direct address for this statement indicates that the Q tradition addresses itself to the "final" generation in which Wisdom's prophetic word of doom is to be fulfilled. The fact that the oracle follows the "woe" against those who "build the tombs of the prophets" (Luke 11:47-48; Matt. 23:29-31) points in the same direction; the oracle is a prophetic proof text which interprets the builders of the prophets' tombs as those who complete the long-foreseen persecution of Wisdom's envoys. Because the oracle is interpolated into sayings which are attributed to Jesus, it is probable that the generation in question is considered contemporary with *both* Jesus and the primitive community which has transmitted the saying.

However, for any Christian community, the list of Wisdom's envoys implied in the *Vorlage* would be incomplete. That is, Zechariah (however he is to be identified) might have served the lost apocalypse as the latest of the persecuted prophets, but he would have provided too remote a terminus to be regarded as a sign of the end for the Christian community. Q can identify the doomed generation as its own (Luke 11:51b, Matt. 23:36) on the grounds that "the blood of all the prophets, shed from the foundation of the world" (Luke 11:50, *cf.* Matt. 23:35) is to be required of it. The end is at hand; the persecution of the prophets has reached its climax. But for this to be proclaimed in a Christian community, it would be necessary to be able to point to one or more recent representatives of Wisdom who have suffered martyrdom and whose death(s) serve as a sign of impending eschatological judgment.

The problem can be illustrated by the alterations made in Matt. 23:34 in order to include members of the Christian fellowship among those whose "righteous blood" has been shed. If Luke was responsible for the term "apostles" (11:49) in his form of the saying, then he was similarly motivated. For Matthew and Luke the passage of time had brought about necessary reinterpretations of the saying. For neither of them could the words "Yes, I tell you, it will be required of this generation" mean what they had meant for Q. By no stretch of the imagination could their generation be regarded as contemporary with Jesus. Therefore, both would have to have been thinking of the persecution of Christians.

However, if the editorial work of the evangelists is removed, there is nothing left in the context in Q to support their interpretation of the oracle—that is, that it refers to the persecution of Christians. When we take into account that the mid-first-century church of which Q is a product might very well have reckoned itself as belonging to "this generation" (that is, to Jesus' own time),[36] then the context of the saying tells us how we are intended to understand it. It is quite clear from both Matthew and Luke that the oracle reached them in connection with material relating to the conflict of Jesus with the scribes. The recently martyred prophet of Wisdom, whose death is a sign of impending judgment, must be the one on whose lips her oracle is placed—Jesus himself.[37] Or, in view of Luke 7:35, we may with probability speak of the two "children of Wisdom," Jesus and John the Baptist, who are rejected by "this generation" (Luke 7:31, Matt. 11:16).

It is important to observe that no effort has been made in Q to introduce any idea of the redemptive significance of the suffering of the representatives of Wisdom. This is in complete accord with the figure of the suffering righteous one in Jewish wisdom and apocalyptic. A picture of this figure is drawn in strong lines in Wisd. of Sol. 2:10—5, a passage which is basically an exposition of the Deutero-Isaianic servant, but which is quite silent with regard to any redemptive significance of his suffering.[38] The righteous man de-

---

36. *Cf.* the early tradition preserved in Mark 9:1 (Matt. 16:28, Luke 9:27) that "there are some standing here who will not taste death before they see the kingdom of God come with power," a saying which must have been firmly fixed in the tradition at a time when the church could think of itself as contemporaneous with Jesus.

37. Tödt, *The Son of Man*, p. 266.

38. See my "Wisdom of Solomon 2:10–5: A Homily Based on the Fourth Servant Song," *Journal of Biblical Literature*, 76 (March 1957), 26–33. One can

scribed in the Wisdom of Solomon actually has no "face." He is not historical, but typical. He certainly is not "Solomon," for the wise king to whom the book is ascribed cannot answer to the description of the suffering righteous one who claims to be a "son of God" in this section. If an attempt is made to identify the figure with Enoch, whose legend may lie behind Wisd. of Sol. 4:10–15,[39] then this only intensifies our impression that the hero is a typical figure; for the experiences reported of the righteous man can only be ascribed to Enoch in so far as he is the type of the righteous. This is further shown by the reappearance of the motif, now with Moses in mind, in the providential history: "For though they had mockingly rejected him who long before had been cast out and exposed, at the end of the events they marvelled at him for their thirst was not like that of the righteous" (11:14);[40] the shaping of the Moses tradition to agree with a typical pattern is apparent. Thus, the suffering of the righteous son in Wisd. of Sol. 2:10—5 is no report of the fate of *a* wise man but a dogmatic statement concerning the destiny of Sophia's ideal representative. Still more important, *the real point of the passage is*, not his suffering and death, but *his vindication*. His humiliation serves no purpose but to show his obedience and the blindness of his persecutors. His exaltation, on the other hand, discloses that his claim to be a son of God and child of Wisdom is true. "At the end" he is a revelation to his persecutors, just as he always was to those who recognized his righteousness and knew that his words were true (Wisd. of Sol. 2:17–18).

It does not appear to me that Q has any other view of Wisdom's martyred prophets. Even the death of Jesus (and John?) is the fate of Wisdom's representative(s). So far as this pericope is concerned, there is no word about vicarious

---

hardly deny that there is a certain "preparation for the gospel" in the few Jewish traditions which speak of the vicarious suffering of the righteous, but in no case are we dealing with a death which is a redemptive event in the sense that the crucifixion was in the Pauline kerygma, for example.

39. So recently U. Wilckens, *Weisheit und Torheit*, p. 173, and Dieter Georgi, "Der vorpaulinische Hymnus Phil. 2, 6–11," in *Zeit und Geschichte*, p. 273.

40. *Cf.* Georgi, "Der vorpaulinische Hymnus," pp. 272–275.

suffering. Jesus is simply the final representative of that line of prophets whose blood is to be avenged. As one sent by Sophia he experiences that rejection which is mankind's repeated response to her message and her messengers. With a fine instinct for the tradition, Matthew prefixes a saying which identifies this generation as the one which "fills up the measure of your fathers." Now, Wisdom's judgment will fall upon them.

It will appear from this analysis that Q is moving in the direction of a Wisdom Christology. Would it be correct to say that such a Christology is present in Q? That question asks more than the examination of one saying can answer. But, in partial anticipation of the investigation of other passages, it may be said that whether one finds a Wisdom Christology in this early Christian source will depend in part on a definition of terms and in large measure on one's assessment of where this material stands in the development of speculation about Sophia towards Gnosticism. If by "Wisdom Christology" one means only that Jesus is here interpreted as Sophia's envoy who brings her truth to men, then the term may be applied. However, if "Wisdom Christology" further implies an advanced Sophia mythology in which Sophia is fully identified with her envoy, then my judgment is that the term is inappropriate. That development must await the manner in which the so-called great church deals with Wisdom speculation; the developed Gnosticism of a later period requires in its background the treatment of Sophia in Paul and in Matthew and in John! What we have in this Q saying is not, properly speaking, Christology at all. It is Sophialogy. As in the gnosticising speculations of Jewish wisdom and apocalyptic literature, so here as well: the ultimate source of revelation is Sophia. Her "prophets, wise men, and scribes" come—with her message.

This is not, of course, the only word which Q has to speak about Jesus. However, in this passage and, as I hope to be able to show, in other sayings as well, the conception of Jesus as Wisdom's final prophet is quite central to Q's proclamation.

28   The subject of this chapter must be pursued further as

Matthew's response to Wisdom speculation in his community is delineated. It is to be hoped that the exploration of Wisdom's oracle of doom (Luke 11:49–51, Matt. 23:34–36) will be allowed to stand as a pointer to the gnosticising potentiality of Q and as the basis for further analysis of Matthew's task as he took this source in hand to incorporate it in his Gospel.

II. Jesus Christ, the Wisdom of God

It has long been recognized that in addition to gnomic sayings the Gospel of Matthew contains two passages which are dependent on Jewish Wisdom speculation. The first, Matt. 11:28–30, is the invitation to men to take upon themselves the "easy yoke." The second, Matt. 23:37–39, contains the so-called lament over Jerusalem, which bears unmistakable traces of the idea of Wisdom's rejection by men.

Treatment of such passages has usually been incidental to some larger concern and has often been relegated to tantalizing footnotes (as in the case of Alfred Loisy).[1] Rarely has an effort been made to regard their testimony as contributing significantly to Matthew's Christology. Edward P. Blair's recent study of the evangelist's Christology does not even have an index entry for Wisdom, although his exposition of the Son of man passages contains suggestive refer-

1. Alfred Loisy, *Les Évangiles Synoptiques* (Ceffonds: Montier-en-Der [Haute-Marne], 1907–1908), 1:913.

ences to Wisdom's place in the Enoch literature.[2] The literature also provides occasional references to other passages, such as Matt. 11:25-27 (the famous "Johannine thunderbolt"), Matt. 11:19 ("Wisdom is justified by her deeds"), and Matt. 23:34-36 (the meaning of which in Q we have already examined). Yet, for the most part, attention has been called to Wisdom themes in Matthew only to designate (and often to dismiss) the key pericopes as erratic outcroppings on the relatively smooth landscape of the Gospel.

There are noteworthy exceptions to this general practice. I have previously referred to James M. Robinson's essays which explore the significance of Sophia speculation in connection with Q; in addition the work of B. W. Bacon, J. A. Findlay, Tomas Arvedson, A. Feuillet, William H. Beardslee, and Ulrich Luck[3] should receive special mention. W. D. Davies is concerned in *The Setting of the Sermon on the Mount* to connect Jewish speculation about Wisdom with the idea of the Messianic Torah,[4] an attempt which, in conjunction with his previous study of Paul, is highly suggestive.

Our purpose is to explore the possibility that a burgeoning current of thought in which Wisdom speculation played a large part made a central, rather than tangential, contribu-

2. Edward P. Blair, *Jesus in the Gospel of Matthew* (New York: Abingdon, 1960), pp. 96–98, 128–129.

3. James M. Robinson, "Basic Shifts in German Theology," *Interpretation*, 16 (January 1962), 76–97; *idem*, "*ΛΟΓΟΙ ΣΟΦΩΝ*: Zur Gattung der Spruchquelle Q," in *Zeit und Geschichte: Dankesgabe an Rudolf Bultmann zum 80. Geburstag,* ed. E. Dinkler (Tübingen: J. C. B. Mohr [Paul Siebeck], 1964), pp. 77–96; B. W. Bacon, *Studies in Matthew* (New York: Henry Holt, 1930), pp. 202–217 and passim; J. A. Findlay, *Jesus in the First Gospel* (London: Hodder and Stoughton, n.d.), pp. 15, 70–86; *idem*, "The Book of Testimonies and the Structure of the First Gospel," *The Expositor*, 8th ser., 20 (1920), 388–400; Tomas Arvedson, *Das Mysterium Christi: Eine Studie zu Mt. 11:25-30* (Uppsala and Leipzig: Lundequistska bokhandeln and A. Lorentz, 1937); A. Feuillet, "Jésus et la Sagesse Divine d'après les Évangiles Synoptiques," *Revue Biblique*, 62 (April 1955), 161–196 (This article was unfortunately overlooked until the present work was virtually complete. Feuillet's approach is affected by his unusual position on the relation of Wisdom and Son of man.); William H. Beardslee, "The Wisdom Tradition and the Synoptic Gospels," *Journal of the American Academy of Religion*, 35 (1967), 231–240; Ulrich Luck, *Die Volkommenheitsforderung der Bergpredigt*, Theologische Existenz Heute 150 (Munich: Chr. Kaiser, 1968), see Chapter Four, n. 8 below.

4. W. D. Davies, *The Setting of the Sermon on the Mount*, (Cambridge, England: Cambridge University Press, 1964), pp. 141–142, 185, and elsewhere. See also his *Paul and Rabbinic Judaism*, 2nd ed. (London: Society for Promoting Christian Knowledge, 1955), chaps. 6 and 7.

tion to Matthean thought. Because the Gospel of Luke provides a measure of literary control in relation to the form of the double tradition, we will focus *primarily* on the Q material in Matthew in anticipation of learning from the evangelist's divergences from the tradition what his distinctive position was. This procedure is adopted because of the "control" provided by Lucan parallels, but it is frankly acknowledged that it results in some distortion. One might easily assume that Q was the only aperture through which Wisdom found her way into the church's life, and that assumption would be mistaken (as Chapter Four will make plain). Moreover, concentrating on Matthew's *divergences* tends to overemphasize the distance between the evangelist and the tradition he has received. That is a danger inherent in the popular and valuable fashion of contemporary scholarship—the fashion of reaching an understanding of a New Testament writer by defining his (frequently, polemic) stance in relation to other currents in the early church.[5] Forewarned of the possibility of distortion in these two directions, the reader may judge whether the method has been justified in this study.

Wisdom's Children and the Children in the Market Place

An unmistakably clear instance of the personification of Wisdom occurs at only one point in the synoptics: Matt. 11: 19b ("Wisdom is justified by her deeds"), a Q saying for which Luke 7:35 provides the more original form, "Yet Wisdom is justified by (all) her children." The logion was in all probability an independent proverb which was introduced into its present location for reasons that the discussion below will indicate.

In its present context in Matthew and Luke the saying about Wisdom's justification is usually understood as a concluding comment on the parable of the children in the market place. Joachim Jeremias appears to regard it as an

---

5. For example, Robinson, "Basic Shifts"; Ulrich Wilckens, *Weisheit und Torheit*, Beiträge zur historischen Theologie 26 (Tübingen: J. C. B. Mohr [Paul Siebeck], 1959); Dieter Georgi, *Die Gegner des Paulus im 2. Korintherbrief*, Wissenschaftliche Monographien zum Alten und Neuen Testament, 11 (Neukirchen-Vluyn: Neukirchener, 1964).

integral part of the parable itself.[6] But this is hardly likely, for the parable is completely self-sufficient without the proverb. The parable proper reads: "But to what shall I compare this generation? It is like children sitting in the market place and calling to their playmates, 'We piped to you, and you did not dance; we wailed, and you did not mourn'" (Matt. 11:16–17, *cf.* Luke 7:31–32). The interpretation of the simile then follows: "For John came neither eating nor drinking, and they say, 'He has a demon;' the Son of man came eating and drinking, and they say, 'Behold, a glutton and a drunkard, a friend of tax collectors and sinners!'" (Matt. 11:18–19a, *cf.* Luke 7:33–34).

Jeremias's paraphrastic interpretation of the passage seems to me completely adequate up to the point where the saying about Wisdom is introduced:

"And you," says Jesus, "are exactly like those domineering and disagreeable children, who blame their companions for being spoilsports because they will not dance to their piping. God sends you his messengers, the last messengers, to the last generation before the catastrophe. But all you do is to give orders and criticize. For you the Baptist is a madman because he fasts, while you want to make merry; me you reproach because I eat with publicans, while you insist on strict separation from sinners. You hate the preaching of repentance, and you hate the proclamation of the gospel. So you play your childish game with God's messengers while Rome burns!"[7]

Precisely! Only this much is needed to expound the parable and its interpretation; the meaning is complete and capable of full understanding without the saying about Wisdom. Jeremias continues, however, with a superfluous reference to God's vindication by his works—that is, to Matt. 11:19—which adds nothing to the parable. The proverb about Wisdom is a secondary interpretation which was already taken up in Q.

6. Joachim Jeremias, *The Parables of Jesus*, tr. S. H. Hooke, rev. ed. (New York: Scribner, 1963), p. 162. So also apparently Norman Perrin, *Rediscovering the Teaching of Jesus* (New York: Harper and Row, 1967), who prints the text of the parable three times, including Matt. 11:19b each time (pp. 85, 105, 119–120).

7. *The Parables of Jesus*, pp. 161–162.

But what does the saying interpret—*only* the parable about the disgruntled children, *or* a longer block of material? Superficially, it would appear to be connected directly and strictly to the parable. If it is limited in this way for the present, what does it mean? The Lucan context, especially Luke 7: 29–30 which speaks of "all the people and the tax collectors" who "justified God," must be ignored. Commentators who find their clue in Luke's own redactional report are apt to interpret "the children of Wisdom" as those who accept Jesus and John. However, Luke 7:29–30 is clearly the evangelist's editorial comment on Jesus' praise of the Baptist. While that comment is important for *Luke's* understanding of the Wisdom saying, it should not be allowed to control any interpretation of the saying so long as the parable is regarded as an independent unit. *So far as the parable itself is concerned, only two sets of principals are involved:* (a) the "men of this generation" who are like spoiled children and (b) Jesus and John. The parable brings no other actors on the scene.[8] The only characters in the pericope who can be regarded as Wisdom's children are, therefore, Jesus and John.[9] If Luke is correct in recording "all her children," then "all" refers to those who belong to the line of Wisdom's envoys. A more detailed examination of the saying will be given later; for the time being, it is enough to observe that the description of John and Jesus as Wisdom's children

8. The tax collectors and sinners of Matt. 11:19a and Luke 7:34 are no more actors in the parable than John's demon in Matt. 11:18, Luke 7:33, and there is no more reason to make them "Wisdom's children" than to include the demon in that category.

9. This discussion obviously assumes that Luke's "children," rather than Matthew's "deeds," belongs to the Q saying. This seems clear to me on the following grounds: (a) The saying was probably attracted to its present location by the presence of children in both the parable ($\pi\alpha\iota\delta\iota\alpha$) and the saying ($\tau\epsilon\kappa\nu\alpha$). (b) The frequency with which "children" appears in the Matthean textual tradition at 11:19 may be due to assimilation of the Matthean text to that of Luke. On the other hand, assimilation in the other direction is what we normally expect, and what we do *not* find here. The assimilation has probably been encouraged, then, by the persistence of the original (Q) form of the saying.

The often-made suggestion that Matthew and Luke present translation variants at this point involves a rather complicated process, and I do not find it convincing. *Cf.* Jeremias, *The Parables of Jesus*, p. 162, n. 44; G. Schrenk, "$\delta\iota\kappa\alpha\iota\omega$," in *Theological Dictionary of the New Testament*, tr. G. W. Bromiley (Grand Rapids: Eerdmans, 1964–   ), 2: 214, n. 13.

requires something like the notion of Wisdom's prophets which we found in Matt. 23:34–36, Luke 11:49–51.

Matt. 11:2–19, Luke 7:18–35—a Unit?

Is it correct to think that in Q the saying was intended *only* to serve as commentary on the parable? This is not to question whether it was related to the parable in Q; that is obvious on the surface. But is it possible that the saying either by itself or in conjunction with the parable was intended to interpret a larger block of material? Certainly, both Matthew and Luke understood it as having a reference beyond the parable.

For Luke, "the children of Wisdom" are no longer Jesus and John, but are those who accept the eschatological messengers. By inserting 7:29–30, Luke has achieved a connection between Jesus' praise of the Baptist (7:24–28) and the parable of the spoiled children (7:31–34). Verse 29 refers directly to what Jesus has just said about the greatness of John in the words "when all the people and the tax collectors heard this," while the phrase "justified God" looks forward to Wisdom's justification by her children. At the same time, the mention in verse 30 of the Pharisees' and lawyers' rejection of God's purpose points unmistakably to the parable which follows. Moreover, Luke (at this point, like Matthew) has taken over from Q a sequential connection (7:24; *cf.* Matt. 11:7) between the story of Jesus' praise of the Baptist and the preceding pericope concerning the question which John sent to Jesus. It would appear, then, that the whole of Luke 7:18–35 is to be taken as a unit of interpretation. The theme of the section in the Third Gospel is man's proper response to the eschatological messengers, Jesus and John. It is punctuated at verse 23 by the saying, "Blessed is he who takes no offense at (Jesus)" and at verse 29 by the observation that by accepting John the people "justified God." It culminates in a parable of warning against those who heed neither Jesus nor John, and the whole is climaxed by the proverb, "Yet Wisdom is justified by all her children" —that is, for Luke, by those who accept these messengers.

36   That Matthew also develops this entire sequence as a block

can, I believe, be shown more quickly and without for the moment addressing ourselves to the question of its meaning in Matthew. The evangelist introduces the section with the clause, "Now when John heard in prison about the deeds of the Christ . . ." The expression "the deeds of the Christ" (τὰ ἔργα τοῦ Χριστοῦ) has an unmistakably technical ring that demands attention. As A. H. McNeile observed, apart from Matt. 1:17, (18?), the title "the Christ" is not employed by itself elsewhere by any of the evangelists in his own material.[10] One would normally expect to find instead something like "Jesus' deeds."[11] The phrase which Matthew has used here surely means something like "the Messianic deeds."[12] Yet, the unusual form τὰ ἔργα τοῦ Χριστοῦ is matched exactly by the Matthean form of the Wisdom saying, which speaks of τὰ ἔργα (τῆς σοφίας). The two phrases serve as brackets for the sequence Matt. 11:2–19.[13]

Bacon correctly regarded the section we have been examining as the longest continuous block of Q material preserved in Matthew and Luke.[14] This fact, coupled with the fact that both Matthew and Luke treat it as a unit of meaning, raises the question whether its function in Q called for such treatment, whether it was a unit in Q as well. T. W. Manson, explicitly, and James M. Robinson,[15] by implica-

10. A. H. McNeile, *The Gospel According to St. Matthew* (London: Macmillan, 1938), p. 151.

11. A "correction" made in some manuscripts including D Sy^c.

12. Krister Stendahl, "Matthew," in *Peake's Commentary on the Bible*, ed. M. Black and H. H. Rowley (New York: Thomas Nelson and Sons, 1962), p. 783, questions whether such a translation would be appropriate. Stendahl does, however, treat Matt. 11:2–19 as a unit.

13. That this is so will become increasingly clear in the subsequent discussion. Prof. Morton Smith has objected in private correspondence that ἔργα "is a very common and colorless word; I doubt that an editor would have felt it sufficient to carry a cross-reference over such a distance [that is, from verse 2 to verse 19]." While I recognize the force of this observation, it also provides an opportunity to underscore the point made above. It is not by the word ἔργα alone but by the unusual expressions τὰ ἔργα τοῦ χριστοῦ and τῶν ἔργων αὐτῆς (τῆς σοφίας) that the connection is made. The frequency with which Matt. 11:2 bobs up in critical comment on 11:19b seems to indicate that the carry-over has been achieved, even when it is not fully understood by modern commentators.

14. *Studies in Matthew*, p. 206 (his "S").

15. T. W. Manson, "The Sayings of Jesus," in *The Mission and Message of Jesus* by H. D. A. Major, T. W. Manson, and C. J. Wright (New York: E. P. Dutton, 1938), pp. 358–363. Robinson, "Basic Shifts," p. 83.

37

tion, regard our passage as the concluding section of the first part of Q. If Lucan order may be presumed to represent the common source, there is much to be said in favor of this proposal. Q has previously introduced John, reported his teaching, introduced Jesus, reported his teaching, and recorded one short account of a healing. Our section thus would stand as a summary which had as its primary purpose the defining of the relation between Jesus and John. If such is the case, then the Q saying about Wisdom and her children/works should be taken as a final comment on the whole section Luke 7:18–35, Matt. 11:2–19 (minus, of course, the evangelists' editorial material).

This does not mean that smaller subunits cannot be discerned in the section or that each of these subunits does not have a special history prior to its incorporation in Q. However, it does mean that the interpreter is bound to try to make sense of the whole *as a whole*, and not simply as casually related bits of independent traditions. Nevertheless, while I am convinced that the entire section forms a unit in Q and will proceed on that basis, the main point I am trying to make does not stand or fall with that assumption. We have already established above the meaning of the logion concerning Wisdom and her children on the hypothesis that the saying is to be related only to the parable of the spoiled children, and the meaning established there is in complete accord with the interpretation which will be developed more fully.[16]

The Children of Wisdom Unit in Q

For Q, the key to the entire section is the concluding proverb: "Wisdom is justified by all her children." Let us

16. The following outline will indicate in what form I believe the material was present in Q.

(a) Luke 7:18–23, Matt. 11:2–6: Both evangelists have edited this paragraph to give it a place in their own Gospels. Q certainly contained the Baptist's question and Jesus' response (with the concluding beatitude).

(b) Luke 7:24–28, Matt. 11:7–11: The parallels between Matthew and Luke in this paragraph are such as to insure that Q has been followed rather closely by both. Luke 7:29–30 and Matt. 11:12–15 are editorial.

(c) Luke 7:31–35, Matt. 11:16–19: While there are significant differences in the wordings of the parable, the only difference important for our purpose is in the appended proverb ($\tau \acute{\epsilon} \kappa \nu \omega \nu$ or $\acute{\epsilon} \rho \gamma \omega \nu$).

review quickly the sequence of the Q report. John the Baptist sends his disciples to inquire if Jesus is the "coming one" (Luke 7:19, Matt. 11:2–3). Jesus answers obliquely by directing their attention to the fulfillment of prophecy in his healing and preaching (Luke 7:21–23, Matt. 11:4–6). When John's disciples have gone, Jesus speaks of the Baptist in a saying which ranks the latter above the prophets of old, assigns him a place of high honor in the divine scheme by naming him as the messenger of the Kingdom (Luke 7:24–28, Matt. 11:7–11), and accords him the rank of greatest born of women. This is followed by the parable of the children playing in the market place (Luke 7:31–34, Matt. 11:16–18), which has as its point the rejection of John and Jesus by the "men of this generation." It is capped by the saying "Wisdom is justified by all her children."

For our interpretation of Q, we should take our cue from the oracle of Sophia found in Luke 11:49–51, Matt. 23:34–36. In our previous examination of the oracle, we found the old idea that Sophia sends her prophets who are rejected by men.

The idea of Wisdom's persistent quest for men by means of her envoys is stated most directly; "in every generation she passes into holy souls and makes them friends of God and prophets" (Wisd. of Sol. 7:27). The fictional "Solomon" addresses the rulers of the world with these words:

> Listen, therefore, O kings and understand;
> learn, O judges of the earth . . .
> Because as servants of his kingdom you did not rule rightly,
> nor keep the law,
> nor walk according to the purpose of God,
> he will come upon you terribly and swiftly . . .
> To you, then, O monarchs, my words are directed,
> that you may learn wisdom and not transgress.
>
> (Wisd. of Sol. 6:1, 4–5, 9)

The point of this typical call to repentance and to the obedience of wisdom is the established motif that by the aid of wisdom "monarchs reign forever." But "Solomon" claims to be able to *mediate* wisdom to men. He is one of those whom Sophia has made "friends of God and prophets."

It is important to identify this Wisdom that is the subject of "Solomon's" discourse. Of course, frequently in the Wisdom of Solomon wisdom is not personified, but is the prosaic and practical rule-of-daily-living familiar at all stages of the wisdom tradition. Yet, in the Wisdom of Solomon the tendency toward the personification of Wisdom reaches a summit. For such passages it is apparent that this is the same Wisdom which is pictured (for example, in Job 28) as inaccessible to men. It is the hidden Sophia of Baruch 3:15; "Who has found her place? And who has entered her storehouses?" It is that Wisdom who says of herself in Sirach 24:4, "I dwelt in high places, and my throne was in a pillar of cloud." She is "a breath of the power of God and a pure emanation of the glory of the Almighty" in Wisd. of Sol. 7:25. As "an initiate in the knowledge of God and an associate in his works" (Wisd. of Sol. 8:4), she "knows the things of old, and infers the things to come; . . . has foreknowledge of signs and wonders and of the outcome of seasons and times" (Wisd. of Sol. 8:8).

Yet, "Solomon" promises those to whom he preaches, "I will tell you what wisdom is and how she came to be, and I will hide no secrets from you" (Wisd. of Sol. 6:22). And he can make this claim because the transcendent Wisdom comes to select men to reveal herself. "She goes about seeking those worthy of her" (Wisd. of Sol. 6:16).

In chapters 10–11 of Wisdom of Solomon, the idea of Sophia's choice of her representatives in successive generations is effectively set forth in relation to Israel's history. The preamble to this recital introduces the succession of Sophia's envoys by saying:

> Who has learned thy counsel, unless thou hast given wisdom
> and sent thy holy Spirit from on high?
> And thus the paths of those on earth were set right,
> and men were taught what pleases thee,
> and were saved by wisdom. (Wisd. of Sol. 9:17–18)

In the following chapters the old *Heilsgeschichte* with its idea of miraculous divine eruption in history is reinterpreted. What is now described is the providential ordering of Israel's history through Sophia's generation-by-generation election of holy servants. Thus, it was Wisdom who guided Jacob "on straight paths and showed him the kingdom of God" (Wisd. of Sol. 10:10), just as she protected Adam, Abraham, and Joseph. In Moses, "she entered the soul of a servant of the Lord and withstood dread kings with wonders and signs" (Wisd. of Sol. 10:16).

It will be important at a later stage to see that the primary medium of revelation, the agent by which Wisdom reveals herself most fully, is the law. This is the particular theme of Sirach. Yet, even in Sirach the individual may serve as Sophia's representative, so that he can say of himself, "I will again make instruction shine forth like the dawn, and I will make it shine afar; I will again pour out teaching like prophecy, and leave it to all future generations" (Sir. 24:32–33).

The language that describes Wisdom's relation to her representatives has a great deal in common with that of mysticism. It is easy, therefore, to apply to this relationship such terms as *synousia*, incarnation, and identification. Rudolf Bultmann insists that such is the relation that "the word of Wisdom's envoy is the word of Wisdom herself."[17] Strictly speaking, modern interpretations in this vein are probably an exaggeration of the intention of the ancient literature. If by "incarnation" one means that Sophia herself takes on an historical form, then it does not appear to me that it can be used accurately of any of her manifestations except the Torah (in which case, I suppose we should speak of an "inliteralization").

Nevertheless, the relation of Sophia to her human representatives is exceedingly intimate. There are, for example, the numerous passages in which Sophia is described as the bride or paramour of her follower. Her representatives may say, "I loved her and sought her from my youth, and I desired her for my bride" (Wisd. of Sol. 8:2); "When I

---

17. Rudolf Bultmann, "Der religionsgeschichtliche Hintergrund des Prologs zum Johannes-Evangelium," "*EYXAPIΣTHPION . . . Herman Gunkel zum 60. Gerburtstage*, ed. Hans Schmidt, Forschungen zur Religion und Literatur des Alten und Neuen Testaments 36 (Göttingen: Vandenhoeck and Ruprecht, 1923), 2: 17 (hereafter cited as *Eucharisterion*).

41

enter my house, I shall find rest with her" (Wisd. of Sol. 8: 16); "He who peers through her windows will also listen at her doors; he who encamps near her house will also fasten his tent peg to her walls" (Sir. 14:23–24). The last of these quotations recalls the personified Wisdom of Proverbs 7 who looks out of her window upon those she would save from the "Harlot" and who in Proverbs 9 invites men to her love feast.[18] That such speculation was widespread in Judaism has now been further confirmed by a Qumran Psalms scroll (11 QPs[a]), which includes a hymn concerning Wisdom of which a bowdlerized version was already known to us in Sir. 51:13–30. The Qumran psalmist speaks of Wisdom coming "to me in her beauty when finally I sought her out . . . I kindled my desire for her without distraction. I bestirred my desire for her, and on her heights I do not waver."[19]

The roles in which Sophia appears as the closest counselor

18. The source of such imagery is in all probability to be sought in the interaction between Judaism and pagan cults in which fertility goddesses peculiarly associated with wisdom were prominent. That one *single* myth of this character is responsible for the development does not appear likely to me. Gustav Boström, *Proverbiastudien* (Lund: C. W. K. Gleerup, 1935), has made a good case for the origin of *certain features* of the Jewish Wisdom figure in a polemic response to an Ishtar cult. Similarly, the Isis aretalogy has been shown (most recently, by Hans G. Conzelmann, "Die Mutter der Weisheit," in *Zeit und Geschichte*, pp. 225–234) to offer interesting parallels to Sirach 24. But the force of Helmer Ringgren's analysis of hypostatizations of divine attributes in the ancient Near East in his *Word and Wisdom* (Lund: H. Ohlssons, 1947) is against attributing the personified figure of Wisdom as such to a well-defined myth of any ancient goddess. Wilckens's effort (in *Weisheit und Torheit* and in *Theologisches Wörterbuch zum Neuen Testament*, ed. G. Kittel and G. Friedrich [Stuttgart: W. Kolhammer, 1933–] 7: 497–528) to describe a proto-Gnostic Jewish Sophia myth which was repressed until it broke out in fresh expression around the beginning of the Christian era is an over-simplification of the history of the figure of Wisdom in Jewish speculation and can only be achieved by reading the evidence in reverse chronological order. A promising approach to this problem was outlined by Burton L. Mack in a paper entitled "Wisdom Myth and Mythology: A Methodological Distinction," read at the annual meeting of the Society of Biblical Literature in Berkeley, California, December 20, 1968. Mack's thesis is that "the employment of the wisdom figure" is "the method by which [a serious] theological concern is expressed and a theological affirmation is made . . . The figure of wisdom becomes the language expression for a category of 'knowledge' which does not belong to man as man on the basis of observation and human experience, but which may now be understood as God's wisdom, a wisdom which stands over against man and confronts him with itself."

19. Col. 21, lines 11–12, 15–17; the translation is that of J. A. Sanders, *The Psalms Scroll of Qumrân Cave 11*, Discoveries in the Judean Desert of Jordan 4 (Oxford: Clarendon, 1965), 81; see also Sanders, *The Dead Sea Psalms Scroll* (Ithaca, N.Y.: Cornell University Press, 1967), p. 115.

of her adherents are multiple. She is also their mother (for example, Sir. 15:2), nurse (11 QPs²), and beloved teacher (Prov. 8:32). The depicting of Sophia as teacher is an expected development, as the school was the home of wisdom. Proverbs 8:32 points to the beginning of a metaphor which developed significance at a later time; in it Wisdom adopts the sage's conventional mode of address to his students, "And now, my sons, listen to me." The metaphor has acquired a richer meaning by the time Sirach writes of the Sage-Mother, "Wisdom exalts her sons" (4:11), or when Q says, "Wisdom is justified by her children."

Yet, in all of this, one finds the nature of this relationship colored by the old prophetic type of inspiration. The representative retains his identity. He speaks for Wisdom, but the "I" of Wisdom remains distinct from his own. Just as the prophet's oracle was marked by a "Thus saith the Lord," so the sage's oracles are characterized by such phrases as "Wisdom cries aloud in the street" (Prov. 1:20), "Does not Wisdom call?" (Prov. 8:1), "Wisdom will praise herself" (Sir. 24:1), "Therefore the Wisdom of God said" (Luke 11:49). Even when he is one of those "holy souls" into whom Wisdom "passes in every generation," the confession of Wisdom's prophet runs like that of "Solomon": "I also am a mortal, . . . in the womb of a mother was I molded into flesh . . . I was nursed with care in swaddling cloths. For no king has had a different beginning of his existence; there is for all mankind one entrance in life, and a common departure" (Wisd. of Sol. 7:1–6). He makes no claim to divine status when he exults, "I called upon God and the spirit of wisdom came to me" (Wisd. of Sol. 7:7b).

Not all men prove to be Wisdom's "children." The idea of Wisdom's coming to men in her messengers is paralleled by the notion of her rejection by men. This side of the story of Wisdom's dealings with men is found in summary in the Johannine indictment, "He was in the world, and the world was made through him, yet the world knew him not. He came to his own home, and his own people received him not" (John 1:10–11). In the oracle of doom of Proverbs 1, Wisdom charges, "Because I have called and you refused to listen" (verse 24). The sermon of Wisdom's scribe, Baruch, is a   43 message calling for Israel's repentance because Israel has "forsaken the fountain of wisdom" (Baruch 3:12), which for the writer means the Torah. 1 Enoch 93:8 tells how "in the sixth week all who live in it shall be blinded, and the hearts of all of them shall godlessly forsake wisdom." Both Sirach and 1 Enoch speak of Wisdom's search for a resting place among men. In Sirach, the search has a happy ending; Wisdom "pitched her tent in Jacob" (24:8) and found "a resting place in the beloved city" (24:11). But the fragment embedded in 1 Enoch 42 reports sadly that Wisdom was forced to return to heaven because she could find no dwelling-place among men.

While one should exercise caution in attempting to draw a clear picture of a single, cohesive myth of the Divine Wisdom from such traces, it is nonetheless possible to draw a generalized picture of Wisdom which is sufficiently articulated to be significant. Even though her characterizations in our diverse sources are still fluid, certain traits are clear. Sophia is a personified entity, with characteristics that are potentially fully mythological. She searches for men with a view to redeeming them. She sends her messengers (who may be individuals or the nation); she is found uniquely in the law. But, tragically, both she and her envoys are rejected by men.

When we set Matt. 11:2–19, Luke 7:18–35 in that context, Q's saying about Wisdom's "children" (Luke 7:35) becomes transparent. Jesus and John are, as the logion implies, Wisdom's representatives. They are, in fact, the eschatological emissaries who, like the emissaries before them, are rejected. Their special significance is determined by the point reached in salvation history. With them, the end is in view. Jesus is the "coming one" and John is "more than a prophet." He who is not offended by Jesus and who recognizes John as the greatest born of women is blessed. But Q must report their rejection by "this generation," which is compared to disagreeable children at play. "Yet Wisdom is justified by her children"—that is, by Jesus and John in whose ministries her righteousness is demonstrated.

If this section is to be so interpreted, the question of the relation of John and Jesus to Wisdom's earlier prophets—

from Abel to Zechariah (Matt. 23:35, Luke 11:51)—
naturally arises. Jesus and the Baptist stand at the turn of the
ages. The references to Jesus as "the one who is to come" and
to John as the eschatological ἄγγελος make this clear. There
can be no doubt that their eschatological functions place
them in a special position. Their unusual status is underlined
by the parable which concludes the section (Matt. 11:16–19,
Luke 7:31–34); the parable pronounces judgment on this
generation because of the rejection of *both* Jesus and John.
Thus, while they belong to the *line* of Wisdom's children, they
occupy a unique place as well. They belong to that event
which the prophets of old "longed to see;" and their proclamation of the inbreaking Kingdom is the message the ancients
"longed to hear" (Matt. 13:16–17, Luke 10:23–24). Therefore, none born of women is greater than John, and those
who are not offended by Jesus are blessed.

The fact that Jesus and John are thus marked off from
their predecessors does not, however, mean that the Q
section under examination treats them as equals. The
subordination of John to Jesus is implied in various ways
throughout the passage. John's question, "Are you he who
is to come?" (Matt. 11:3, Luke 7:19) suggests the Baptist's
anticipation of one greater than himself and prepares in
advance for the pericope's concluding beatitude (Matt. 11:
6, Luke 7:23).[20] The next paragraph (Matt. 11:7–11a, Luke
7:24–28a) appears at first reading simply to provide Jesus'
unlimited endorsement of the Baptist. The title "prophet"
seems to be regarded as an inadequate designation of the
Baptist; he is "more than a prophet" (Matt. 11:9–10, Luke
7:26–27). At whatever point the quotation from Mal. 3:1
entered into the tradition, it is a proof text appended to the
description of John as "more than a prophet." The citation
from Malachi interprets the phrase "more than a prophet"
in line with the prophecy: "This is he of whom it is written,
'Behold, I send my ἄγγελον.'" Of course, it would be rash to
translate ἄγγελος as "angel." But the use made of the Old

20. This is true whether "the coming one" is interpreted messianically or as a
reference to the "eschatological prophet" (*cf.* Oscar Cullmann, *The Christology of
the New Testament*, tr. S. C. Guthrie and C. A. M. Hall, 2nd ed. [London: Student
Christian Movement Press, 1963], p. 26).

Testament quotation requires us to understand that John is not only a prophet: he is that once-translated Elijah whose return as a special *messenger* has been promised. The Apocalypse of Weeks specifically connects Elijah's translation with the repudiation of Wisdom's message: "And after that in the sixth week all who live in it shall be blinded, and the hearts of all of them shall godlessly forsake wisdom. And in it a man shall ascend" [that is, Elijah] (1 Enoch 93:8). What is reported in Q is the "second coming" of Wisdom's representative Elijah, who is now recognized as being "more than a prophet." The exaltation of the Baptist does not reach its climax in the quotation from Malachi, however. Jesus himself is called to witness that "among those born of women there has arisen no one greater than John the Baptist" (Matt. 11:11a, Luke 7:28a).

As soon as this climactic word in praise of John is spoken, another element is introduced that demands attention. For now we read, "Yet he who is μικρότερος in the kingdom of God is greater than he" (Luke 7:28b, Matt. 11:11b). Largely on the basis of this verse, this section has been regarded as anti-Baptist polemic, that is, as polemic against a sect in which John was reverenced more highly than Jesus.[21] That such a polemic eventually emerged in the life of the Church, the Fourth Gospel constitutes eloquent testimony, but that a sectarian bias of this kind is to be found in Q is exceedingly doubtful. As W. D. Davies has argued, "Q was not concerned with polemic against John's followers but with the crisis which he announced to be impending."[22] The quotation from Mal. 3:1 would only make nonsense otherwise. To be sure, if one follows the interpretation which reads at this point, "Yet he who is *least* in the kingdom of heaven is greater than he," then the polemic understanding is all but unavoidable. In that form, it can hardly mean other than "John is born of a woman," and he who is born "not of blood

21. Martin Dibelius, *From Tradition to Gospel*, tr. B. L. Woolf (New York: Scribner, 1935), p. 244, and *The Sermon on the Mount* (New York: Scribner, 1940), pp. 17–18, is usually cited approvingly in this connection.

22. *The Setting of the Sermon on the Mount*, p. 369. *Cf.* Robinson, "Basic Shifts," p. 84: "One may recall that it is in Q that one has a surprisingly high evaluation of John, for in sharp contrast to Mark and the Gospel of John Q gives to the Baptist's own non-Christological message an importance in its own right."

nor of the will of the flesh nor of the will of man" (John 1:13) or he who is born "of water and the Spirit" (John 3:5–8) is greater than he; that is to say, any Christian is greater than John.[23] The Gospel of Thomas (Saying 46), in fact, has this saying in a form that requires such an interpretation: "From Adam until John the Baptist there is among those who are born of women none higher than John the Baptist so that his eyes will not be broken. But I have said that whoever among you becomes as a child shall know the Kingdom and he shall become higher than John."[24]

Yet, as Cullmann has observed,[25] a mistranslation of the Greek is necessary to wrest this meaning from Q, which should be read, "The *lesser* (of the two) is greater than he in the kingdom." Translated in this fashion, the saying acknowledges that Jesus was at one time the "lesser," the disciple; it also claims for Jesus higher rank in the Kingdom. But the saying is not intended to detract from the high status bestowed on the Baptist in the preceding verses. In fact, it really does no more than is already implied in the Malachi quotation—which Q employs both to exalt him as the ἄγγελος and to explain John's merely temporal priority in terms of his *heilsgeschichtlich* role as forerunner. One is tempted to say that the whole of Matt. 11:2–11, Luke 7:18–28 contains a subtle subordination of the Baptist; but there is really

23. Prof. Morton Smith, in private correspondence, calls attention to John 3:5–8 as a possible alternative to being "born of woman." The Johannine passages represent a particular development and are, of course, only illustrative.

24. Antoine Guillaumont, H.-Ch. Puech, G. Quispel, W. Till, and Yassah 'Abd Al Masih, eds. and trs., *The Gospel According to Thomas* (Leiden and New York: E. J. Brill and Harper, 1959), p. 27.

25. Oscar Cullmann, "The Significance of the Qumran Texts for Research into the Beginnings of Christianity," *Journal of Biblical Literature*, 74 (1955), 219, reprinted in *The Scrolls and the New Testament*, ed. K. Stendahl (New York: Harper, 1957), p. 24. See also his "Ο ΟΠΙΣΩ ΜΟΥ ΕΡΧΟΜΕΝΟΣ," In honorem Antonii Fridrichsen Sexagenarii, Coniectanea Neotestamentica 11 (Lund and Copenhagen, 1947), 26–32, translated in Cullmann's *The Early Church*, ed. A. J. B. Higgins (Philadelphia: Westminster, 1956), pp. 177–182. Cf. F. Blass and A. Debrunner, *A Greek Grammar of the New Testament and Other Early Christian Literature*, tr. and rev. Robert W. Funk (Chicago: University of Chicago Press, 1961), p. 33.

By "mistranslation" is not meant that μικρότερος can only be a comparative; in certain contexts, it is a superlative. The Q context, however, is so completely dominated by its interest in Jesus and John that it does not so much as hint at who some "least" one could be, and the comparative is required. Discussions of this point with my colleagues, George P. Fowler and John W. Stewart, have been of great value to me.

nothing subtle about it. Q only reports the faith of a community for which John's significance was great— and Jesus' was greater.

This concern reaches a crest in the concluding pericope— the parable of the spoiled children and its application to Jesus and John (Matt. 11:16–19a, Luke 7:31–34). In its original form this saying about Jesus and John was one in which they were treated as equals.[26] As we have already observed, it pronounces judgment on this generation, not because of the rejection of Jesus alone, but because of the rejection of John, as well. However, in the Q form of the saying, Jesus is given the august title "Son of man." Although condemnation continues to fall on those who reject both of Wisdom's final prophets, this title again ascribes to Jesus a rank above that of John. To declare that he is Son of man is to speak of him as indissolubly connected with the last judgment.[27]

Son of Man and Sophia in Q

Yet, the naming of Jesus as Son of man is not an alternative to recognizing him as a child of Wisdom, for the Son of man is closely associated with wisdom. This has been shown quite clearly in a cautious article by James Muilenberg.[28]

26. So Jeremias, *The Parables of Jesus*, p. 160, n. 37. Jeremias is also correct in thinking that the saying must be very early since the church consistently subordinates John to Jesus. However, his attempt to retain the words "Son of man" in the original saying by giving it a special meaning is not likely to be correct; see also Perrin, *Rediscovering the Teaching of Jesus*, p. 120. A. J. B. Higgins, *Jesus and the Son of Man* (London: Lutterworth, 1964), pp. 122–123, quite properly rejects "Son of man;" he prefers the simpler explanation of "the presence of the Son of man in this undoubtedly genuine utterance" as "the result of early Christian interpretation of an original I-word."

27. See Higgins, *Jesus and the Son of Man*, pp. 119–142, 185–192; H. E. Tödt, *The Son of Man in the Synoptic Tradition*, tr. D. M. Barton (London and Philadelphia: Westminster, 1965), esp. pp. 47–67, 114–125. It is important to stress that our concern is not with whether or not any class of Son of man sayings originated with Jesus. It is only in certain instances that we must determine whether the present formulation of a particular saying is to be attributed to the church at a particular moment in the history of the tradition.

28. James Muilenberg, "The Son of Man in Daniel and the Ethiopic Apocalypse of Enoch," *Journal of Biblical Literature*, 79 (1960), 197–209. Muilenberg mentions "exaggerations, questionable parallels, and above all serious omissions" in connection with the attempt to establish a close relation between Messiah, Wisdom, and Son of man by A. Feuillet in "Le Fils de l'homme de Daniel et la tradition biblique," *Revue Biblique*, 60 (1953), 170–203; 321–346.

Muilenberg speaks of the "numerous affinities between apocalypse and wisdom," and mentions specifically "what the wisdom literature has to tell us about the more or less hypostatized wisdom." He recognizes the importance of sacral kingship ideology in relation to the Son of man, but suggests "that the prophetic passages concerning the sacral king are woven into the context of wisdom speculation."[29]

The picture of the Son of man in the Similitudes of Enoch[30] (1 Enoch 37–71) is painted on a surface on which wisdom influences are prominent. "In him [that is, the Son of man] dwells the spirit of wisdom, and the spirit which gives insight, and the spirit of understanding and might" (49:3). "His mouth shall pour forth the secrets of wisdom and counsel" (51:3). There is a strong emphasis on wisdom throughout the Similitudes. Indeed, the superscription of the collection speaks of the "vision of wisdom—which Enoch . . . saw . . . the beginning of the words of wisdom . . . such wisdom [as] has never been given by the Lord of Spirits" (37:1–4). The place in which the Son of man is "named" is filled with fountains of wisdom from which the thirsty "drink and [are]

29. *Journal of Biblical Literature*, 79 (1960), 207, 208, cf. 204.

30. The absence of Similitudes fragments from the Enoch materials uncovered at Qumran has become for many scholars a respected argument from silence against the use of the Similitudes as a part of the background of the synoptic Son of man tradition. This seems to me to be unfortunate, since silence is so difficult to interpret, and all the more so since the genuine problems of dating the Similitudes are obscured by this consideration. I think the problems remain essentially the same and that the Similitudes are pre-Christian. This, it seems to me, is the simplest explanation of the striking correspondences between the two Son of man figures.

Of recent attempts to dispose of the Similitudes as a part of synoptic backgrounds, two illustrate the complexity these correspondences introduce into alternative hypotheses. N. Perrin, *Rediscovering the Teaching of Jesus*, pp. 164–199, finds that use of a "Son of man imagery" based on Daniel 7 was made *independently* by the "scribe(s) of the Similitudes of Enoch to interpret the translation of Enoch, and by those of early Christianity to interpret the resurrection of Jesus" (p. 198). Because translation to the status of Son of man is involved in both instances, surely a shared exegetical tradition (at the very least) explains the correspondences better than spontaneous, independent development. And, if there was such a tradition, then there was an apocalyptic, Jewish Son of man conception.

J. C. Hindley, "Towards a Date for the Similitudes of Enoch: An Historical Approach," *New Testament Studies*, 14 (1968), 551–565, argues that certain "historical" references in the Similitudes are best matched by a date shortly before A.D. 120 (Trajan's expedition in the East in 113–117 and an earthquake in Antioch in 115). But, for Hindley, the correspondences between the Similitudes and the synoptics leads to the suggestion that the Enochian Son of man is anti-Christian polemic!

filled with wisdom" (48:1). Moreover, it is even said that the Son of man has been revealed "to the holy and righteous by the wisdom of the Lord of Spirits" (48:7). H. L. Jansen's study of the Enoch tradition stresses repeatedly the relation of the Son of man to wisdom; it is Jansen's view that Ea-Oannes, the Babylonian god of wisdom, furnished the model of the Son of man.[31]

Does this mean that for Q Jesus is viewed as the pre-existent Son of man who has come to earth and will return to his heavenly residence? There is, so far as I can see, no evidence that the Son of man speculation in Q is associated in any way with the figure's pre-existence.[32] To be sure, Jesus is made to say at this particular place (Luke 7:34, Matt. 11:19), "The Son of man has come." Yet this in itself is a conventional, prophetic claim. There is no saying in Q which speaks of the heavenly pre-existence of the Son of man. On the contrary, the verses which speak of the future Son of man have in view Jesus's exaltation to that status.[33] This reminds us of the idea of the translation of outstanding holy men—for example, Enoch, Elijah, and Moses.[34] It does not appear unlikely that 1 Enoch 70–71 regards the Son of man as the exalted Enoch.[35] Indeed there may be some relation between this idea and the judgment scene of 1 Enoch 62, in which the confounding of the kings and mighty of the earth by the appearance of the Son of man shows striking correspondences with the vindication of the righteous son in Wisdom of Solomon.

The Son of man belongs with Wisdom. The attribution of this title to Jesus constitutes further evidence that for Q he is the greatest of Wisdom's representatives. But even this does not mean that Jesus has displaced Wisdom in Q. Rather,

31. H. L. Jansen, *Die Henochgestalt, eine vergleichende religionsgeschichtliche Untersuchung* (Oslo: J. Dybwad, 1939), pp. 105, 108–111.

32. Tödt, *The Son of Man*, pp. 284–292, denies that pre-existence is present in any of the synoptic Son of man passages.

33. The point at issue here is not what such futuristic sayings might have meant in their original form. The point is that, once Jesus was specifically identified in his earthly existence as the Son of man, there is no trace that Q ascribed that status to him on the basis of a doctrine of pre-existence.

34. For example, Jub. 4:23, 1 Enoch 93:8.

35. See M. Black, "The Eschatology of the Similitudes of Enoch," *Journal of Theological Studies*, n.s., 3, (1952), 1–10.

the concluding saying of this section (Luke 7:35—"Wisdom is justified by [all] her children.") still places him in the line of Wisdom's prophets, even though the larger context obviously assigns to him and in somewhat lesser measure to John the Baptist a position of pre-eminence among the prophets.[36]

The Q tradition retains at another place a saying which probably should be interpreted as subordinating the Son of man to Sophia. This is the troublesome logion: "And every one who speaks a word against the Son of man will be forgiven; but he who blasphemes against the Holy Spirit will not be forgiven" (Luke 12:10, cf. Matt. 12:32).[37] This saying invites consideration at this point if only because the accusation that the "Son of man is a glutton and drunkard, a friend of tax collectors and sinners" might very well be understood as a "word spoken against the Son of man."

It is not easy to imagine a situation in the life of the early church in which blasphemy against the Son of man would be regarded as forgivable. The direction in which recent scholarship has moved in an effort to come to terms with this saying may be indicated by two quotations. Higgins thinks:

As an independent saying it referred to the difference between those who spoke against the Son of man from outside the church

36. Cf. T. Preiss, "Jésus et la Sagesse," Études Théologiques et Religieuses, 28 (1953), 70.

37. The saying is paralleled in Mark 3:28-29, Didache 11:7. Helmut H. Koester, Synoptische Überlieferung bei den apostolischen Vätern, Texte und Untersuchungen 65 (Berlin: Akademie, 1957), 215-217, probably is correct in the opinion that Did. 11:7 is essentially independent of both the Mark and Q traditions, thus witnessing to the wide and persistent circulation of variant forms of the saying. It is not clear to me, however, as it is to Koester, that "in der Did. die ursprünglichere Form und Anwendung dieser Regel vorliegt" (p. 217). The saying in the Didache has lost much of its eschatological force and has become "domesticated" as a genuine ecclesiastical rule for judging the trustworthiness of prophets.

As to whether Q or Mark is more original, I am inclined to favor Q—although the concurrence of T. W. Manson ("The Sayings of Jesus," 401-402) and R. Bultmann (The History of the Synoptic Tradition, tr. John Marsh [New York: Harper and Row, 1963], p. 131) on the side of Mark is enough to make me uneasy. Yet, it is incredible to me that a saying like that in Q could arise as a result of mere misunderstanding.

However the question of the temporal priority of the various forms of the saying is settled, we must still come to terms with its meaning in Q. And in Q, the saying regards blasphemy against the Spirit as more serious than a word spoken against the Son of man. (Saying 44 of the Gospel of Thomas presents a still more radical position: even blasphemy against the Father may be forgiven!)

51

and apostates within who sinned against the Holy Spirit . . . Be
that as it may, the fact that the *Son of man* is an object of blasphemy
establishes the Palestinian provenance of the saying, and so it is not
hostile outsiders in general who are intended but the Jews . . . The
attitude of the church would have been that blasphemy against the
Lord, serious though it was, could be forgiven those Jews who were
converted and came in baptism to confess Jesus as the exalted Lord
and Son of man.[38] [Emphasis in original.]

Tödt comments along these lines:

. . . the saying states that opposition to the Son of Man can be forgiven, but opposition to the Holy Spirit cannot. Here, too, the
name Son of Man does not designate the figure of a transcendent
Perfecter, but in accordance with Matt. 11.19 and par. it designates Jesus acting on earth and being attacked by his opponents . . .
They can be forgiven in so far as they turned against the Son of
Man merely in his activity on earth. But there is no forgiveness—
in the post-Easter situation—for the one who sets himself in
opposition to the manifest activity of the Holy Spirit. Two periods
in the history of salvation are distinguished here in the saying from
Q, the period of Jesus' activity on earth as the Son of Man and the
subsequent period of the activity of the Holy Spirit. The meaning
of the distinction is quite intelligible. In the Spirit the exalted Lord
reveals himself.[39]

The weakness of these interpretations is that both obviously
strain to avoid the surface significance of the saying, namely,
that the Son of man is regarded as in some sense inferior to the
Spirit. Both, but especially Tödt, are too much under the
spell of the tripartite division of Son-of-man sayings (earthly
ministry, passion, future glory), which has made possible
their proposed solution to the problem of the originality of
the sayings. While neither would insist that his analytical
categories were the theological categories of the early church,
both suppose that at this point the problem of the "word
against the Son of man" can be solved by thinking in terms
of the distinction between the Son of man in his earthly
activity and the Son of man as exalted Lord. What they really
want the logion to say is this: "Every one who speaks a word

38. *Jesus and the Son of Man*, p. 130.
39. *The Son of Man*, p. 119.

against Jesus may be forgiven, but he who blasphemes against the exalted Lord may not be forgiven." Now, while something like this may *approximate* Matthew's understanding of the saying, Q is lacking the requisite doctrine of the Spirit to support this interpretation. What is needed is a word like Paul's "the Lord is the Spirit" (2 Cor. 3:17), and this Q does not supply. An alternative interpretation is called for.

We are confronted by a shocking circumstance: Q acclaims Jesus "Son of man"—and yet regards blasphemy against him as a less serious sin than blasphemy against the Spirit. As Robin Scroggs has said:

> There is no suggestion in the logion, once it is separated from its Matthean context, that the "Son of man" means Jesus before his resurrection. The Son of man is probably rather the *coming* Lord; thus the saying accentuates the primacy of the Spirit with bold audacity.[40]

Such an audacious evaluation of the Spirit is met at only one other point in early Christian literature, namely, in those pneumatics against whom Paul directs the judgment in 1 Cor. 12:3, "Therefore I want you to understand that no one speaking by the Spirit of God ever says 'Jesus be cursed!' and no one can say 'Jesus is Lord' except by the Holy Spirit." It is more than interesting that it is precisely in that community where "Sophia" and "Spirit" had become catchwords of a gnosticising spiritualism, where Christians wore tags like "Paulinists" and "Cephasites" (1 Cor. 1:12), where Paul decided to "know nothing among you except Jesus Christ and him crucified" (1 Cor. 2:2)—that it is precisely in this community that men possessed by the Spirit claimed the freedom to pronounce an anathema on Jesus.[41]

40. Robin Scroggs, "The Exaltation of the Spirit by Some Early Christians," *Journal of Biblical Literature*, 84 (1965), 364. Scroggs also quite properly recognizes that efforts to establish the Matthean setting as original are largely motivated by the desire to discover "a more historically justified location in the ministry of Jesus" (p. 362). The Matthean setting is simply that of Mark. While the Lucan context is not an entirely happy one, the preceding Son of man saying in 12:8–9 at least provides a basis for catchword association. Since we cannot fix on either Matthew or Luke as providing the Q setting of the logion, it is best to treat it independently.

41. On this passage, see Scroggs, *Journal of Biblical Literature*, 84 (December 1965), 365–373; Robinson, "Basic Shifts," p. 85; and Walter Schmithals, *Die Gnosis in Korinth*, Forschungen zur Religion und Literatur des Alten und Neuen

In both Q and 1 Corinthians we are confronted by pneumatics who claim an immediate and intimate relation to the Spirit which renders their allegiance to Jesus secondary. In 1 Corinthians Paul promulgates church law against them, but in Q we meet the inspired legal pronouncement of the pneumatics themselves: blasphemy against the Son of man is serious (it must be forgiven), but blasphemy against the Spirit cannot be forgiven.

This situation is rendered fully intelligible by the association of Wisdom and Spirit in late Judaism. Frequently, this association shows dependence on the messianic passage in Is. 11:2, where every attribute assigned to the Spirit of the Lord is connected with wisdom, "the spirit of wisdom and understanding, the spirit of counsel and might, the spirit of knowledge and the fear of the Lord." Thus in 1 Enoch 49:3, the spirit which dwells in the Elect One is the "spirit of wisdom, insight, understanding, and might." As is well known, the identification of Sophia and Spirit is made complete in Wisdom of Solomon (cf. 1:6–7; 7:22; 9:17). The figure who dominates the providential history of Wisd. of Sol. 10–11, which we have previously mentioned, is demonstrated by 9:17 to be just this Wisdom-Spirit.

Thus, while in Matt. 11:18–19, Luke 7:33–34 the introduction of the title "Son of man" subordinates John to Jesus, we may not assume that for Q the title takes Jesus out of the line of Wisdom's children. He, like John before him, like the prophets before John, is sent by Wisdom—the heavenly revealer who retains her priority even over the Son of man.

Testaments 66 (Göttingen: Vandenhoeck and Ruprecht, 1956), 45–50, 138–140. However, it is *not* our contention that "blasphemy against the Son of man" implies Schmithals' contrast of the "human Jesus" and the "Pneumachristus." On the contrary, the identification of Christ with Sophia-Pneuma is a Pauline and Matthean development. In Q (and among the so-called Corinthian Gnostics) Jesus is regarded as only a representative of Sophia; Sophia is the supreme revealer, whom to anathematize is unforgivable. Birger Pearson, "Did the Gnostics Curse Jesus?" *Journal of Biblical Literature*, 86 (September 1967), 301–305, correctly argues that Schmithals' use of *Contra Celsum* 6:28 is not a legitimate comparison with 1 Cor. 12:1–3, but he also acknowledges that the question of the meaning of 1 Cor. 12:1–3 is quite independent of the problem of the Origen text (p. 305).

On the general subject of the relation of Q to 1 Corinthians, see Robinson, "Basic Shifts," pp. 85–86, and "Kerygma and History in the New Testament," in *The Bible in Modern Scholarship*, ed. J. P. Hyatt (Nashville and New York: Abingdon, 1965), pp. 128–130.

It is not a digression from our long-range objective to introduce here a further, brief word concerning the title "Son of man" in Q. Because the title is associated with predictions of Jesus' suffering in some strata of the synoptic tradition, it might be suggested that reference to Jesus as Son of man in this passage introduces a concern for the passion. Both Higgins and Tödt[42] have demonstrated that Q knows nothing about a "suffering Son of man." Whether they are justified in concluding from this fact that sayings which connect the Son of man with the passion of Jesus are late developments is not quite certain. Q reports nothing of substance concerning the passion outside the Son of man sayings, either. It must at least be admitted as a possibility that a theological bias is at work in the whole Q tradition which operates against the inclusion of passion material. In any case, the title in Matt. 11:19, Luke 7:34 is no "back door" through which a concern for the cross may be smuggled!

Here then is the second and final summary of my interpretation of the Q section given in Matt. 11:2–19, Luke 7:18–35. Jesus and John stand as the eschatological envoys of Wisdom. Their position in relation to the eschaton gives them special status: John is Elijah, Jesus is the Son of man. They, like the emissaries who preceded them, are rejected. It would thus appear that this section of Q has been so constructed as to find its summation in the concluding logion, in which—as Bultmann argued long ago—the phrase "children of wisdom" designates "the Baptist and Jesus as envoys of Wisdom, as prophets."[43]

The Children of Wisdom Unit in Matthew

When we turn to the editorial activity of Matthew to determine the evangelist's use of this section, we are struck first of all by the deceptively slight alterations which have been made. That the changes are so few may be attributed to Matthew's acceptance of Sophia speculation as a legitimate vehicle of Christian proclamation. Luke's editorial activity

---

42. Higgins, *Jesus and the Son of Man*, chap. 8; Tödt, *The Son of Man*, esp. pp. 246–253.

43. *Eucharisterion*, p. 15; *cf.* Wilckens, *Theologisches Wörterbuch zum Neuen Testament*, 7:516.

has taken the entire passage out of the context of wisdom thought altogether. Matthew's changes have no such effect. The section continues to be about Wisdom, her representatives and her rejection. Nevertheless, Matthew's alterations are not inconsequential. His modifications bring about a re-interpretation of far-reaching importance.

The most noteworthy change occurs in the concluding proverb, Matt. 11:19b. Here, Matthew has replaced "Wisdom is justified by [all] her children" with the sentence, "Wisdom is justified by her deeds" (ἀπὸ τῶν ἔργων αὐτῆς). Along with this alteration, it is important to recognize the evangelist's editorial introduction to the section, which speaks of "the deeds of the Christ" (τὰ ἔργα τοῦ χριστοῦ). That the unusual expression "the deeds of the Christ," of which we have previously spoken, is editorial is shown by the fact that χριστός is not a Q designation of Jesus. Nor can there be any doubt that Matthew intends these "Messianic deeds" to be central to the whole section, Matt. 11:2–24. Note that Matt. 11:20–24, the woes against the Galilean cities, is provided with an elaborate transition which reads: "Then he began to upbraid the cities where most of his mighty works had been done, because they did not repent." As Georg Strecker observes, with reference to Matt. 11:2, 19, 20, "The mighty deeds of Jesus prove the right of his claim, which is the claim of the divine Sophia."[44] The fact that verses 2 and 19 speak of "deeds" (ἔργα) while verses 20–24 speak of "mighty works" (δυνάμεις) does not at all detract from the connection which Matthew intends to make. Matthew reports the "works" as a part of the "deeds." As Held has demonstrated, the "deeds" of verse 2 include the "mighty works" which have been reported in chapters 8–9, and also the "words" of chapters 5–7, and the missionary commission of chapter 10.[45] When Matthew speaks of the

---

44. G. Strecker, *Der Weg der Gerechtigkeit*, Forschungen zur Religion und Literatur des Alten und Neuen Testaments 82 (Göttingen: Vandenhoeck and Ruprecht, 1962), p. 102.

45. H. J. Held, "Matthew as Interpreter of the Miracle Stories," in Günther Bornkamm, Gerhard Barth, and H. J. Held, *Tradition and Interpretation in Matthew*, tr. P. Scott (Philadelphia: Westminster, 1963), pp. 250–253; *cf.* G. Bornkamm, "Der Auferstandene und der Irdische, Mt. 28, 16–20," in *Zeit und Geschichte*, p. 185, n. 58.

" deeds of Wisdom " in verse 19b and of the " might works "
performed in Galilee in verses 20–24, he is not speaking
about two different things; nor is he speaking about one
single type of activity which requires the use of the same word
in both places. He is, rather, speaking of the " mighty works "
as one dramatic manifestation of the broader category
" Messianic deeds " or " deeds of Wisdom."

If this is true, then when Matthew speaks of the " deeds of
the Christ," " the deeds of Wisdom," and " mighty works "
performed in Galilee, he is always talking about this one
thing: the deeds of Jesus.[46] And the plain implication of this
fact is that Matthew has consciously modified the saying
about " Wisdom's children " into one about " Wisdom's
deeds " *in order to identify Jesus with Wisdom*. In this way, Jesus
is no longer the last and greatest of Wisdom's children; in
him are the deeds of Wisdom to be *uniquely* seen. Matthew's
qualification of the speculation which lies behind this passage is this: a succession of prophets have been inspired by
Wisdom, of whom the greatest is John; but it is now a matter
of Wisdom's absolute and unqualified appearance in Jesus
Christ. For Q, Wisdom sends forth her prophets—from the
first generation to this generation which has rejected Jesus
and John. However, it would not greatly overstate the case
to say that *for Matthew* Wisdom has " become flesh and
dwelled among us " (John 1:14).

Viewed in this manner, the reason for Matthew's insertion
of 11:12–15 becomes clear.[47] Whatever is to be made of the
dark saying concerning " violence and the Kingdom," this
much seems plain: with John the Baptist the " new " has
erupted into history.[48] John stands at a dividing point; the

---

46. *Cf.* Feuillet, *Revue Biblique*, 62 (1955), 167–168.

47. Once it is seen that the material in Matt. 11:2–19, Luke 7:18–35 is derived
from *a unit in Q*, it is difficult to see how Matt. 11:12–15 can be regarded as a part
of the Q-unit. Matthew successfully integrates the saying about violence and the
kingdom into the section by the addition of the clearly editorial verses 14–15.
Without these verses, Matt. 11:12–13 (parallel, Luke 16:16) is no longer a saying
that fits the theme of the relation of Jesus and John, and it interferes with the
material connection between Matt. 11:11 and 11:16. The saying about violence
and the kingdom was doubtless in Q, where (as in Luke) it was concerned solely
with the relation of John's preaching of the kingdom to the law and the prophets.

48. Ernst Käsemann, *Essays on New Testament Themes* (London: Student
Christian Movement Press, 1964), pp. 42–43.

fulfillment of prophecy sets in with him, for he is "Elijah who is to come." Matthew's intention is to fix John the Baptist's place in this Wisdom *Heilsgeschichte* more specifically, to clarify by repetition his significance as Elijah, and to reinforce by this specific identification John's subordination to Jesus. John 1:6–8 is a polemically extended commentary on the Baptist which throws light on Matt. 11:12–15, "There was a man sent from God whose name was John. He came for testimony, to bear witness to the light, that all might believe through him. He was not the light, but came to bear witness to the light." Matthew intensifies both Q's exaltation of John and Q's subordination of the Baptist to Jesus, but he is no more motivated than was Q to combat the "Baptists." His quarrel with Q is purely over the status assigned to Jesus in relation to Wisdom.

With Matthew, the attempt to relate Jesus to Sophia has moved to a new stage. What we find in Q is "Sophialogy." To be sure, we can add on the basis of this section (as we could not in discussing Matt. 23:34–36, Luke 11:49–51) that a Christology related to speculation about Wisdom has appeared in Q. However, it is a Son-of-man Christology, and for Q even the Son of man is subordinate to Sophia. It is here that Matthew moves in a different direction. His alterations in chapter 11 show that, for him, Sophia is *identified* with Jesus. Jesus is Sophia incarnate.[49]

Wisdom's Oracle of Doom in Matthew

It is now possible for us to return to the subject of Wisdom's oracle of doom (Luke 11:49–51, Matt. 23:34–36). In the

49. This is an appropriate place to indicate my understanding of the direction in which the Wisdom speculation is moving. The speculation in Q stands on a line which extends from the Wisdom of Solomon to the "prophetic succession" of the pseudo-Clementines. What we find in Matthew (the identification of Jesus with Wisdom) moves in two directions: toward the Christology of the early Fathers, on the one hand, or toward the developed Gnosticism of (for example) the Acts of Thomas, on the other; neither development is intelligible apart from the identification of Christ and Sophia which occurs first in Paul, Matthew, and John. *Cf.* H. Koester's review of Wilckens' *Weisheit und Torheit* in *Gnomon*, 33 (September 1961), 590–595, which properly stresses that it is precisely Paul, not his opponents, who identifies Christ and Wisdom. Robinson, "Basic Shifts," pp. 85–86, thinks that "only in Q and I Corinthians is Sophia clearly a Christological title." Our point is that Sophia is a *Christological* title in Matthew and Paul, *not* in Q or among Paul's opponents. See also Robinson, *The Bible in Modern Scholarship*, pp. 129–130.

preceding chapter, our examination of this section led to the conclusion that the oracle had been taken up by Q from a lost Jewish source; in Q it tells of the sending of Sophia's prophets and their rejection—including the rejection of the martyred Jesus.

Matthew's alterations are, again, slight but significant. Matthew turns Q's Wisdom saying into a dominical oracle. Just as Matthew can on occasion substitute the personal pronoun for the title "Son of man" (for example, Matt. 5:11) and vice versa (for example, 16:13), because for him Jesus and the Son of man are one; so at this place the evangelist puts Wisdom's words on Jesus' lips.[50] He no longer retains the formula, "Therefore also the Wisdom of God said, 'I will send them prophets'" (Luke 11:49), but writes instead, "Therefore I [Jesus] send you prophets." In his *Das Wahre Israel*, Wolfgang Trilling argues that the substitution of the ἐγώ of Jesus for "the Wisdom of God" is Matthew's way of "actualizing" the text. In a certain sense this is true, but in such immediate proximity to Matt. 23:37–39, which reports Wisdom's rejection by Jerusalem, and in the light of what we have already observed about Matthew's use of the saying in 11:19, one cannot interpret this "actualizing" so as to support Trilling's declaration that it is "not advisable to draw Christological consequences from the replacement of Sophia by Jesus."[51] On the contrary, it must be recognized that in making this change Matthew has assigned to Jesus Wisdom's function as the sender of prophets—a function which belongs to no figure in pre-Christian Judaism except Wisdom and God, so far as I can see. Trilling's statement that the prophets are sent "not by God's Wisdom, but by Jesus" misses the point of Matthew's alteration. By this substitution Matthew has transferred to Jesus an activity which is specifically

50. *Cf.* Strecker, *Der Weg der Gerechtigkeit*, p. 124, n. 11.

51. So in the first edition of Wolfgang Trilling's *Das Wahre Israel*, Erfurter Theologische Studien 7 (Leipzig: St. Benno, 1959), 63. But in the third edition (in Studien zum Alten und Neuen Testament 10 [München: Kösel, 1964], 81) the sentence has been removed. *Cf.* Douglas R. A. Hare, *The Theme of Jewish Persecution of Christians in the Gospel According to St. Matthew*, Society for New Testament Studies Monograph Series 6 (Cambridge, England: Cambridge University Press, 1967), p. 140, n. 3: "The daring Christological claim implicit in 23:34 ought not to be overlooked."

characteristic of Wisdom—namely, the commissioning of prophets and scribes.

Furthermore, while the suffering of Jesus' disciples is anticipated on the basis of their following Jesus in his way, it should be stressed that Matthew's accommodation of the language of the oracle to cover the persecution of members of the Christian community in no way removes the saying from its original ideological environment; the predicted suffering of Christian prophets remains the persecution and rejection of Wisdom's envoys. Matt. 5:12 specifically includes Jesus' disciples in the prophetic line, in a saying which implies by its solemn, "So men persecuted the prophets who were before you," that the suffering of the disciples is a continuation of the agelong rejection of the messengers of heaven.

Thus, like Q, Matt. 23:34–36 records an oracle of Wisdom, in which it is promised that prophets will be sent forth and it is predicted that they will suffer. Their suffering will lead to the judgment of "this generation." For Matthew only two refinements must be made: the term "prophets" is extended to include disciples of Jesus, and Jesus is again identified with Wisdom.

The recognition that Matthew responded in just this way to a kind of Christian message in which Christ was understood as a messenger of Wisdom, but in which Wisdom herself was still regarded as the supreme revealer figure, brings to mind again the situation confronted by Paul in 1 Corinthians. Helmut Koester, in a review of U. Wilckens's *Weisheit und Torheit*, properly denies that the identification of Sophia with Christ has been made by Paul's opponents. Koester proposes the possibility that the apostle's opponents thought of Christ "as the bringer of wisdom, or as the 'sage,' although not as 'Wisdom' itself," just as Philo spoke of Moses as mystagogue, teacher, and hierophant.[52] He makes the important point that it was precisely Paul who made the identification of Wisdom and Christ! If the situation in Corinth is understood in this fashion, then Matthew and Paul were confronted by similar (not, of course, identical) forms of Wisdom speculation. Both responded by making an express

52. Koester, *Gnomon*, 33 (1961), 594.

identification of Christ and Wisdom against opponents for whom Jesus was but one of Wisdom's envoys. The examination of Matt. 11:2–19 and 23:34–36 in this chapter confirms that Matthew altered the Q material with this end in view.[53]

Matthew's attitude toward the speculation about Wisdom is ambivalent. To the extent that it introduces a revealer to whom Jesus is subordinated, he is drawn into combat against it. On the other hand, by daring to advance Jesus as incarnate Wisdom, he is able to modify the speculation and to use it for his own purposes. Further modifications will be observed in the subsequent discussion, and it will gradually become clear why Matthew chose to alter rather than abandon the speculation.

---

53. Andor Szabó, "Anfänge einer judenchristlichen Theologie bei Matthäus," *Judaica*, 17 (1960), 193–197, 201–202, attempts to understand Jesus in relation to this saying as "der höchste Prophet." But the article as a whole seems to me methodologically anachronistic; the martyr theology and syzyge doctrine which Szabó finds requires beginning where Szabó begins: with the pseudo-Clementine literature. The Q saying represents a line of thought that may stand behind the pseudo-Clementines, but Matthew must not be interpreted from this perspective.

III. Jesus Christ, God's Wisdom and God's Son

We turn now to a consideration of the familiar lament over Jerusalem, a Q passage preserved almost identically in Matt. 23:37–39 and Luke 13:34–35 and which is correctly identified as a Wisdom logion.[1] It reads:

O Jerusalem, Jerusalem, killing the prophets and stoning those who are sent to you! How often would I have gathered your children together as a hen gathers her brood under her wings, and you would not! Behold, your house is forsaken! And I tell you, you will not see me until the time comes when you say, "Blessed be he who comes in the name of the Lord!"[2]

1. Rudolf Bultmann, "Der religionsgeschichtliche Hintergrund des Prologs zum Johannes-Evangelium," in *EYXAPIΣTHPION*, Forschungen zur Religion und Literatur des Alten und Neuen Testaments 36 (Göttingen: Vandenhoeck and Ruprecht, 1923), 2: 6; U. Wilckens, "σοφία, σοφός," in *Theologisches Wörterbuch zum Neuen Testament*, ed. G. Kittel and G. Friedrich (Stuttgart: W. Kohlhammer, 1933–) 7: 516.
2. On the form of the final sentence, see below, n. 22.

In the Gospel of Luke, the saying is found immediately following the pericope which reports Jesus' response to the information that Herod is seeking Jesus to kill him (13:31–33). The response concludes with the exclamation, "it cannot be that a prophet should perish away from Jerusalem!" In Matthew, it follows right upon the heels of Wisdom's oracle of doom over those who persecute and kill the "prophets, wise men, and scribes."

The Location of the Lament in Q

It is not certain that either evangelist has retained the Q-setting of the saying. Both *could* have placed the passage in their own contexts on the basis of mere *Stichwort* association, since the preceding pericope in Matthew also speaks of the killing of prophets, while in Luke the lament follows directly after a sentence in which the words "Jerusalem" and "prophet" are used. However, the saying is really too important in its present location in both Gospels for keyword association to be accorded first consideration in this matter, and the choice between the two settings on this score alone is too even to be decisive.

Bultmann was convinced that the Matthean setting is the original context in Q—and, in fact, that Q preserves here the order of the postulated wisdom-apocalypse which may be the *Vorlage* of both the doom oracle and the lament.[3] In favor of this position is the probability that both sayings are to be understood as words of Sophia. Moreover, Luke's location artistically, if not artificially, prepares the way for the fulfillment of the words, "You will not see me until the time comes when you say, 'Blessed be he who comes in the name of the Lord,'" at the time of the triumphal entry (see Luke 19:38).[4] In this way, the preceding saying in Luke becomes a summary statement rounding out the Galilean period, while the lament sets the tone for the journey to Jerusalem. The theological utility of the story's position in Luke's general

---

3. R. Bultmann, *The History of the Synoptic Tradition*, tr. John Marsh (New York: Harper and Row, 1963), pp. 114–115; James M. Robinson, "Basic Shifts in German Theology," *Interpretation*, 16 (January 1962), 84.

4. *Cf.* William C. Robinson, Jr., *Der Weg des Herrn*, Theologische Forschung 38 (Hamburg, 1964), p. 54.

development thus provides a negative argument in favor of the Matthean setting.

Yet, objections have been raised to its present location in Matthew, as well. E. Haenchen pointed out that while in the doom oracle "the 'Wisdom of God' looks forward prophetically to the future sending of the prophets," in the lament "she looks back on the sending of the prophets."[5] The force of this objection is somewhat weakened by the fact that in keeping with its form the doom oracle almost requires a future tense, while the dirge form of the lament equally requires the past. However, the fact that the sayings are different in *form* has been set forward by both Haenchen and T. W. Manson[6] as an objection to the connection of the two sayings in Q and/or the wisdom source. Once again, I do not find this connection of differing forms—doom oracle followed by dirge—an insuperable difficulty, although the absence of any transition does create an impression of abruptness. Haenchen further objects that it is difficult to explain Luke's removal of the lament to another location, if it originally followed the doom oracle; difficult as it is, we cannot deny that Luke's purpose would have been so admirably served by the removal as to make it comprehensible. Manson's argument that the saying is found in a Lucan context which is largely comprised of Q material[7] is weakened by the observation that neither the

5. E. Haenchen, "Matthäus 23," *Zeitschrift für Theologie und Kirche* 48 (1951), 56.

6. T. W. Manson, "The Sayings of Jesus," in *The Mission and Message of Jesus* by H. D. A. Major, T. W. Manson, and C. J. Wright (New York: E. P. Dutton, 1938), pp. 418–419.

7. "The Sayings of Jesus," p. 394. W. G. Kümmel, *Promise and Fulfillment* (London: Student Christian Movement Press, 1957), pp. 80–81, also separates Matt. 23:37–39 from the preceding oracle (verses 34–36) on what I think are insufficient grounds: (1) Luke is not "given to tearing apart passages belonging together in his sources." (But it is obvious that Luke has not preserved the sequence of his sources in this section, whether he is "given to" this practice elsewhere or not.) (2) The "second passage is not really a continuation of the first." (I assume that this is an argument based on form like that of Haenchen and Manson discussed above.) (3) *Sophia* as the speaker in Luke 11:49 cannot be original, because in Matthew "Jesus appears as the sender of prophets," and Matthew's thought is too unusual to be secondary. (Are we really to assume that Luke rejected Jesus as the sender of "prophets and apostles" in order to introduce Sophia in that role?) (4) Why, Kümmel asks, would Matthew "change the σοφία in Luke into the σοφοί sent by Jesus?" (Why would Luke change the σοφοί sent by Jesus into σοφία who sends prophets and apostles?— is the reverse, and more difficult, question.) (5) Matt. 23:37–39 need not "be ascribed to a mythical being," but could have been spoken by Jesus. (That, of course, is a matter of opinion. It is always possible that a pattern appropriate to a "mythical"

preceding nor the following pericopes in Luke can be assigned to Q with complete confidence; in fact, Luke 14–15 is composed of alternating blocks of Q and special source material.[8]

On the whole, in spite of the stylistic jar provided by the attaching of two sayings of such different form, it appears most probable that Matthew preserves the Q order.

The Meaning of the Lament in Q

The saying cannot be attributed to Jesus. The sentence, "How often would I have gathered your children together as a hen gathers her brood under her wings," is in itself sufficient proof of that. The metaphor requires a heavenly, indeed, a divine being. Thus, a passage of Christian origin that may be dependent on our saying reads: " [Thus says the Lord Almighty: . . .] I gathered you as a hen gathers her brood under her wings" (2 Esdras 1:30). In at least eight places[9] in the Old Testament, a similar allusion to the "wings of God" appears—although in a vast majority of cases in a cultic context where the "wings" in question may actually be the wings of the seraphim; the idea regularly seems to be that his wings are a place of protection. In the Syriac Apocalypse of Baruch 41:3–4, the unfaithful are said to have "cast from them the yoke of Thy law," while the faithful have "fled for refuge beneath Thy wings." The unwillingness of the Rabbis to use the name of God in this way probably accounts for the fact that they speak of the conversion of a proselyte as "bringing him under the wings of the Shekinah."[10] The connection between Wisdom and the Shekinah in such diverse Wisdom passages as John 1, Sirach 24, and Proverbs 8 was noticed long ago by Rendel Harris,[11] and Strecker is

being would be used by a historical individual; but is it ever *probable?*) Kümmel devotes pp. 79–82 to a brief and clear discussion of the passage and his footnotes furnish a helpful bibliography.

8. This fact about Luke 14–15 was called to my attention by H. Koester.

9. Deut. 32:11; Ruth 2:12; Ps. 17:8, 36:7, 57:1, 61:4, 63:7, 91:4.

10. See H. L. Strack and P. Billerbeck, *Das Evangelium nach Matthäus*, Kommentar zum Neuen Testament aus Talmud und Midrasch 1 (München: C. H. Beck, 1922), p. 931 (on Matt. 23:15).

11. J. R. Harris, *The Origin of the Prologue to St. John's Gospel* (Cambridge, England: Cambridge University Press, 1917); for our passage, the Wisdom-Shekinah connection is also noticed by T. Preiss, "Jésus et la Sagesse," *Études Théologiques et Religieuses*, 28 (1953), 70.

careful to point out that in the lament "Jesus occupies the place of the Shekinah."[12] Tomas Arvedson remarks apropos of our verse that it is obvious "that the picture of the bird with its young is thoroughly appropriate in the mouth of maternal Sophia."[13]

In view of the fact that the remainder of the pericope accords so well with what is known of the portrait of Wisdom in Judaism, I shall assume that the speaker in this pericope was, in Q, Sophia.[14] It can be properly attributed to Jesus *only* when the step is taken which Matthew makes in the preceding pericope, that is, when Wisdom and Jesus are identified.[15] Matthew intends the saying to be understood as a word of incarnate Wisdom whom he sees in Jesus.

At the beginning of the lament, Wisdom is heard bemoaning the murder of her envoys—the prophets whom we recognize by now as sent "in every generation" to issue the call to repentance and knowledge. The tenderness of her intention then comes to expression; she "would have gathered your children together like a hen gathers her brood under her wings." It is always clear in the Wisdom literature that Sophia offers her revelation to men with wistful longing for their acceptance. In Proverbs 8 she "calls," she "raises her voice," "by the paths" and "at the gates;"

> To you, O men, I call
> and my cry is to the sons of men.
> O simple ones, learn prudence;
> O foolish men, pay attention. (verses 4–5)
> I love those who love me,
> and those who seek me diligently find me. (verse 17)

12. G. Strecker, *Der Weg der Gerechtigkeit*, Forschungen zur Religion und Literatur des Alten und Neuen Testaments 82 (Göttingen: Vandenhoeck and Ruprecht, 1962), p. 113.

13. Tomas Arvedson, *Das Mysterium Christi: Eine Studie zu Mt. 11:25–30* (Uppsala and Leipzig: Lundequistska bokhandeln and A. Lorentz, 1937), p. 211.

14. Considered purely from the point of view of content, the saying might also be attributed to God. However, in view of the prominence of Wisdom in Q and of Matthew's understanding of the passage (see immediately below), this does not appear probable to me.

15. Luke, of course, improperly attributes it to Jesus.

67

According to the Wisdom of Solomon, "she goes about seeking those worthy of her, and she graciously appears to them in their paths" (6:16). In 1 Enoch 42:2 she "went forth to make her dwelling among the children of men." Sirach 24 tells how Sophia "sought a resting place," a territory in which she "might lodge" (verse 7). This Wisdom hymn in Sirach is of special importance for our passage, for it tells how the Creator commanded her to "make her dwelling in Jacob," so that she "ministered before him in the holy tabernacle" and found a resting place in Jerusalem, "the holy city" (verses 8–12). It is presupposed in our passage that Wisdom's earthly abode is the temple in Jerusalem.

Yet, it is precisely in Jerusalem that "the prophets and those sent to you" have been killed. Wisdom's graciousness is rejected. Therefore, the lament continues to its climax, "Behold, your house is forsaken!"[16] The same circumstance is reflected in John 1:11, where it is said of the Logos that "he came to his own home, and his own people did not receive him." Thus, Baruch 4:12 reports a lament by Jerusalem in which the city cries:

> Let no one rejoice over me, a widow,
>   and bereaved of many;
> I was left desolate because of the sins of my children,
>   because they turned away from the law of God.

This passage in Baruch is significant for the understanding of our passage. The punishment of Jerusalem in both the Q saying and in Baruch is attributed to the rejection of Wisdom. To be sure, Baruch causes Jerusalem to say, "I was left desolate . . . because they turned away from the law of God." However, this statement is probably to be understood in terms of Baruch 4:1, where Wisdom is specifically identified

16. I leave open the question of the inclusion of ἔρημος. It is attested for Luke 13:35 by several important witnesses (D lat syᶜ Iren. Or. Eus.). Although ἔρημος is lacking from B L ff² syˢ sa bo at Matt. 23:38, its attestation by such divergent and important witnesses as C D W f. 1 f. 13 it vg is impressive. And, since the "captivity" theme seems to be important in several accounts of Wisdom's rejection and is strengthened by the word's presence, it probably should be regarded as original. If so, as an allusion to Jer. 22:5, it would furnish an added point of contact with Baruch 4:12, discussed immediately below.

with the Torah in the words:

> [Wisdom] is the book of the commandments of God,
>   and the law that endures for ever.
> All who hold her fast will live,
>   and those who forsake her will die.

The marked apocalyptic tone of both the oracle of doom and the lament[17] recalls a passage from 4 Ezra (5:9b–10), belonging to a context which enumerates eschatological signs: "Then shall reason hide itself, and wisdom shall withdraw into its chamber, and it shall be sought by many but shall not be found, and unrighteousness and unrestraint shall increase on earth." Perhaps such apocalyptic prediction furnishes the setting for the previously mentioned interpolation in 1 Enoch 42, which speaks of Wisdom returning to heaven after vainly seeking a dwelling-place among men.[18]

Haenchen regards the last verse of the saying as a Christian addition, because "Wisdom was non-existent in persona in previous time" and it is inappropriate therefore to speak of "not seeing" her again.[19] In his view, therefore, the pre-Christian saying ended with the pronouncement of judgment: "Behold, your house is forsaken." It is not easy to see the force of this argument, as it is clear that Wisdom (like the Shekinah) was conceived of as "dwelling" in the temple and might, in keeping with the "captivity" motif, be conceived of as deserting the temple.[20] However, the fact that the

17. K. Stendahl, "Matthew," in *Peake's Commentary on the Bible*, ed. M. Black and H. H. Rowley (New York: Thomas Nelson and Sons, 1962), p. 793, remarks: "With this verse [32] the style changes to that of an apocalyptic oracle which concludes the discourse against the Pharisees at the same time as it leads over to (37–9) the prediction of Jerusalem's destruction and the apocalypse proper (ch. 24)."

18. Alternatively, 1 Enoch 42 reflects an older "Wisdom myth" and 4 Ezra 5:9b–10 shows its adaptation in Jewish apocalypse; *cf.* U. Wilckens, *Weisheit und Torheit*, Beiträge zur historischen Theologie 26 (Tübingen: J. C. B. Mohr [Paul Siebeck], 1959), pp. 160–162, and *Theologisches Wörterbuch zum Neuen Testament*, 7: 508–509 (and on its relation to Matt. 23:37–39, p. 516). This is perhaps possible. However, it is most attractive when one ignores the fact that in both 1 Enoch and 4 Ezra Wisdom's vain search for a dwelling is followed by a note to the effect that "Unrighteousness" has its way with men. This addition shows that in both cases Wisdom is probably already identified with the Torah.

19. *Zeitschrift für Theologie und Kirche*, 48 (1951), 57.

20. Klaus Baltzer, "The Meaning of the Temple in the Lukan Writings," *Harvard Theological Review*, 58 (July 1965), 272–273, seems to suggest that both

quotation from Ps. 117:26 was in use in the early church may be an indication that the verse has been added in Q.[21] If so, then it was appended in a community where the Wisdom speculation was well understood.[22] Bultmann is then correct in his opinion that "Wisdom foretells that she will remain hidden until the coming of the Messiah."[23]

The Lament in Matthew

Matthew's most significant alteration in the passage occurs in this verse. The lament's connection with the doom oracle shows that Matthew regards it as a Wisdom word as well. For Matthew, Jesus is incarnate Wisdom, and the evangelist therefore both historicizes the final verse and gives it a specific reference to the Parousia by writing: "For I tell you that from

---

Wisdom and the kābôd may stand behind our passage. He thinks that, in view of Ezek. 11:23, "it may not be only a coincidence that Mt. 24:3 finds Jesus at the Mount of Olives."

21. See Bultmann, *History of the Synoptic Tradition*, p. 115.

22. Barnabas Lindars, *New Testament Apologetic* (London: Student Christian Movement Press, 1961), p. 173, properly regards ἔως ἥξει ὅτε εἴπητε (D, Luke 13:35) as the original reading in Q, since it best explains the other variants. "This means that ὁ ἐρχόμενος is a different person from the speaker," in Lindars's opinion. Attractive as this suggestion is, K. Stendahl (in a private communication) has convinced me that this opinion cannot be justified on *grammatical* grounds alone. See F. Blass and A. Debrunner, *A Greek Grammar of the New Testament and Other Early Christian Literature*, tr. and rev. Robert W. Funk (Chicago: University of Chicago Press, 1961), pars. 382(2), 381(1); A. T. Robertson, *A Grammar of the Greek New Testament in the Light of Historical Research*, 4th ed. (New York: Hodder and Stoughton, 1923), pp. 971–976.

That ὁ ερχόμενος is a person other than the speaker is assured, however, on the grounds already presented: the lament is a lament of Sophia and the final sentence of the lament is to be so interpreted (even if it is a Christian addition). For Q, as argued above, Wisdom speaks of a "time when" which is eschatological. Luke interprets historically by placing the saying at a point in his Gospel where the future reference can be fulfilled by the entry into Jerusalem.

Matthew, who has fully identified Jesus with Wisdom, alters the construction at the outset. Since for him Jesus and Sophia are one, Matthew substitutes for ἔως ἥξει ὅτε εἴπητε the words ἀπ' ἄρτι ἔως ἂν εἴπητε—and, in this way, both emphasizes Jesus' separation from the temple and city and points to the Parousia. 'Απ' ἄρτι is a characteristic Matthean expression; it appears three times in the first Gospel, never in Mark and Luke. See also Matt. 26:29, 64, where ἀπ' ἄρτι appears to be an editorial addition to Marcan material. (On Matt. 26:64, J. A. T. Robinson, *Jesus and His Coming* [London: Student Christian Movement Press, 1957] pp. 48–49, thinks ἀπ' ἄρτι was already in Mark 14:62, although the textual evidence in favor of this position is unimpressive.)

23. *History of the Synoptic Tradition*, p. 115.

this time on you will not see me until you say, 'Blessed is he who comes in the name of the Lord.'" That is, Matthew successfully transfers a Wisdom saying to Jesus because for him Jesus is identified with Sophia. It is in Wisdom's person that Jesus can speak of "how often" in relation to Jerusalem, for the call of Wisdom has been heard again and again in "the prophets and those sent;" the "how often" has nothing to do with the number of trips made to Jerusalem by the historical Jesus, but with how Wisdom in every generation has appealed to men through her prophets and has not been heeded. As this figure, Jesus can say—as no merely historical individual might—"I would have gathered your children under my wings." Jesus is Wisdom incarnate.

Thanksgiving and Revelation

We must turn now to another passage which has been frequently identified as having affinities with Jewish Wisdom literature,[24] Matt. 11:25–27, which is translated by RSV in the following form:

At that time Jesus declared, "I thank thee, Father, Lord of heaven and earth, that thou hast hidden these things from the wise and understanding and revealed them to babes; yea, Father, for such was thy gracious will. All things have been delivered to me by my Father; and no one knows the Son except the Father, and no one knows the Father except the Son and any one to whom the Son chooses to reveal him."

The Problem of the Text (Matt. 11:27, Luke 10:22)

Since the work of Adolf Harnack it has been necessary to consider carefully the textual problems attendant to verse 27

24. Reference should be made here to André Feuillet's treatment of this passage in "Jésus et la Sagesse Divine d'après les Évangiles Synoptiques," *Revue Biblique*, 62 (1955), 169–196, and now also to his *Johannine Studies*, tr. T. E. Crane (Staten Island, N.Y.: Alba House, 1965), pp. 98–102. Feuillet makes many of the points which are advanced below. However, he holds a number of basic judgments which I do not share, so that it would be misleading to cite him in support of specific points in my own argument: (1) his exegesis requires that Matt. 11:25–30 be a unit; (2) the unit is regarded as a genuine saying of Jesus; (3) the identification of "Son of God" with "Son of man" and "Wisdom" is pre-Matthean (indeed, it was achieved prior to Jesus' ministry). At the same time, his insights into the related wisdom materials are exceedingly valuable.

and its Lucan parallel (10:22).[25] The evidence bearing on the original text of the saying has been painstakingly gathered by Paul Winter, who concludes that the manuscript tradition has preserved only a corrupt form.[26] The article discusses what Winter calls "the six main problems" in the passage. Of these, two make no substantial difference to the sense of the saying, and another is of only minor importance. We cannot avoid giving consideration to the remaining problems.

The first has to do with the opening clause: "All things have been delivered to me by my Father." At the outset we become immediately aware of the degree to which Winter has conceived the problem so as to bring together issues of a very different kind. The question is whether in the original we are to read "*my* Father" with the bulk of the manuscript evidence or if we are to read instead "*the* Father" with certain witnesses. Now there can be no question that the evidence favoring the omission of the pronoun "my" before "Father" is quite strong for Luke—including Codex Bezae, the Sinaitic Syriac, three Old Latin manuscripts, several Vulgate witnesses, and several early Fathers. But the situation is quite different with respect to Matthew. In Matthew, the omission is found in the first hand of Codex Sinaiticus, three minuscules, and *perhaps* three Fathers. Winter discusses as a block the patristic evidence in favor of the omission—whether it bears on the text of Luke or of Matthew, a procedure which unaccountably assumes that the original text of both Gospels was identical at this point. For Matthew, only one of two citations from Justin seems to be applicable; that from Hippolytus is obviously made *memoriter* and may, therefore, reflect his memory of Luke; Hilary's quotation is problematic. I am inclined to think that Luke may have had "the Father" rather than "my Father;" and, if so, this may also be what was found in Q. However, from a purely textual point of view, the weight of the evidence for the Matthean form of the verse seems to be on the side of the inclusion of the pronoun "my."

This problem illustrates the tendency of Winter to ignore

25. Adolf Harnack, *New Testament Studies II: The Sayings of Jesus*, tr. J. R. Wilkinson (New York: G. P. Putnam's Sons, 1908), pp. 19–20.

26. Paul Winter, "Matt. xi. 27 and Luke x. 22 from the First to the Fifth Century: Reflections on the Development of the Text," *Novum Testamentum*, 1 (1956), 112–148.

the fact that we have to do here with *two* Gospels which have separate histories. He repeatedly assumes that the same factors have operated to bring about almost identical alterations independently to both Gospels. Although the evidence for omission in Matthew is not strong and even though Winter himself observes that "Matthew frequently adds a μου to ὁ πατήρ in Sayings of Jesus where Mark or Q had no μου," Winter concludes that "μου did not stand in the original text of either Matthew or Luke."[27] I can see no justification for this assumption. With respect to the omission or inclusion of the pronoun "my," it appears to me that it would be sounder to view the matter in some such fashion as this. Luke originally omitted the pronoun, while Matthew included it. Later, assimilation of Luke to Matthew resulted in the addition of the pronoun to most Lucan manuscripts, while in a few cases Matthew was assimilated to Luke by its omission.

Two of Winter's problems may be considered together, as they have to do with the following clauses: "[a] And no one knows the Son except the Father, [b] and no one knows the Father except the Son." Is this the original *order* of the clauses? Does [a] belong in the text?

In spite of the fact that Luke's form of this saying diverges significantly from Matthew's, Winter chooses to discuss the evidence on these two clauses indiscriminately. He has gathered the evidence for Matthew and Luke *separately* at the beginning of his article, but he tends to develop his argument as if the witnesses to the Matthean text are also witnesses to Luke, and vice versa. That is, his discussion does not take into account that when two uncials (N and X) support the "reversed" order for Matthew, and two Greek manuscripts (N and U) and one old Latin manuscript (b)[28] support

---

27. *Novum Testamentum*, 1 (1956), 128 and 128, n. 2.

28. In collecting the evidence at the beginning of the article, Winter mistakenly gives Latin manuscript *o* as a witness to the inverted order in Luke; see *Novum Testamentum*, 1 (1956), 126. Eldon J. Epp has reminded me that H. S. Cronin, *Codex Purpureus Petropolitanus*, vol. 4 in Texts and Studies 5 (Cambridge, England: Cambridge University Press, 1899), p. xlvii, believed that in N the inverted order was accidental both at Matt. 11:27 and at Luke 10:22. The accident occurred when a scribe inserted πατήρ and υἱός into the wrong spaces (the spaces having been left for gold lettering). Cronin considers this "less obvious" for Matthew than for Luke, but "not less certain."

it for Luke, he is dealing with evidence bearing on two different documents. Nor does he point out that patristic evidence in support of the "reversed" order is much stronger for Matthew than for Luke. Instead, in his exposition of the problem, the Matthean and Lucan evidence is lumped together. One is tempted to suppose that Winter is really seeking to settle a source- or tradition-critical question by the use of text-critical analysis. Yet his "survey of results" makes it clear that it is the history of the text—indeed, the "historical changes in the formation of the canonical text"—which is his interest. This makes it all the more surprising when he seeks to nail down his most important opinion—namely, that the statement "no one knows the Son except the Father" is not original in either Matthew or Luke—by appealing finally to the purely formal analysis of C. F. Burney.[29] Once again, it appears to me that the issue cannot be settled properly along these lines. I think that the traditional order was original at least in Luke. I am inclined to prefer the traditional order for Matthew, but less confidently than for Luke.

Whatever our judgment of the traditional order, it is necessary to deal with Winter's (and Harnack's) proposal concerning the non-genuineness of the phrase concerning the Father's knowledge of the Son. In the first place, Winter acknowledges that the clause is included in every known straight-text Greek manuscript, in all the Fathers, and in every witness to the versions save one. It is not found in the Latin Codex Vercellensis (a) at Luke 10:22—an omission that may be due to a scribal blunder only. That is a slender peg on which to hang so heavy a garment! We are asked to believe that neither Matthew nor Luke had the clause originally, that both were altered (either independently or one in dependence on the other) to include a clause they did not originally possess, and that the only direct evidence of the original text which remains for us is to be found in a fourth-century Latin manuscript. Now, anyone familiar with the vagaries of the transmission of the text will acknowledge that

29. *Novum Testamentum*, 1 (1956), 146–148; *cf.* C. F. Burney, *The Poetry of Our Lord* (Oxford: Clarendon, 1925), pp. 171–172.

this is not wholly inconceivable. Indeed, if only one Gospel were involved, a handful of examples could be garnered to illustrate this type of phenomenon. But one would have to extend credulity to the limits to believe that the "scholarly labour to lay down an officially approved text"[30] was so unusually persistent and effective in respect to this particular pericope as to achieve such near-perfect results in the case of two different documents whose textual histories are by no means identical. Of course, Winter himself acknowledges that "it would hardly be prudent to base a conclusion on the exceptional text of Codex Vercellensis."[31]

Therefore, he argues (quite correctly) that "the great majority of early patristic quotations gives" the saying about the Son's knowledge of the Father *after* the clause "all things have been delivered to me by the Father." This is true, and constitutes incontrovertible proof that the early Fathers were accustomed to quoting the passage with the second and third clauses in the reverse of the order we know from the manuscript tradition. This certainly indicates something. It indicates that *either* the patristic *or* the manuscript tradition is at fault.

But does the evidence indicate that (as perhaps at Matt. 5:5) the trouble is an otherwise undetected interpolation into the Matthean and Lucan texts? Winter thinks this is the answer, and he appeals somewhat sarcastically to "the small matter of logic."[32] He objects that it just is not logical to say what is declared in the saying: "*If the Son is unknown to anyone* except the Father, *how can the Son reveal the Father to others?*"[33] [Emphasis in original.]

Whether the canons of logic ought to be applied to a revelation saying in just this manner is doubtful. Even so, Winter's argument breaks down as soon as he tries to translate the final line. For, literally, that line (in both Matthew and Luke) reads: "And any one to whom the Son chooses to reveal." That is, the infinitive ἀποκαλύψαι is used absolutely

30. Winter, *Novum Testamentum*, 1 (1956), 135.
31. *Novum Testamentum*, 1 (1956), 129.
32. *Novum Testamentum*, 1 (1956), 129.
33. *Novum Testamentum*, 1 (1956), 130.

—either without an object or with an object to be supplied. Indeed, he admits that if the supplied object is "himself" rather than "him" then "line 3^b *can* follow upon the former two lines, but we would have to understand the whole verse in the sense: 'Nobody knows the Father but the Son and nobody knows the Son but the Father and he to whom the Son wishes to reveal *himself*.'"[34] This, as he says, is logical; but he never pursues its possibility because it is at variance with the interpretative tradition. Thus, he provides one avenue of escape from his own trap.

Also, one wonders if perhaps the verb "reveal" should be given a special, esoteric significance at this point and the clause translated: "And any one to whom the Son chooses to give a revelation." Or, more promisingly, we could perhaps accept the hint provided by the other absolute use of "reveal" in Matthew's Gospel, at 16:17, and render the line "and anyone to whom the Son reveals *this* or *these things*." The latter suggestion would be particularly attractive since it would provide reference back to the "all things delivered to me" at the beginning of the verse. Thus, if logic drives us inexorably away from anything, it is away from the traditional interpretation of the last clause as meaning "and anyone to whom the Son chooses to reveal him."

We are, for the moment, arguing on Winter's grounds, and presuming that the kind of logic which he proposes is normative for our understanding of the passage. Even on these grounds, it is not correct to add, as he does, that the saying must mean the same thing whether the phrase about the Son's knowledge of the Father comes first or last before the concluding clause.[35] If the text of Matthew witnessed to by the early Fathers is correct, then it is entirely possible that the concluding clause should be interpreted as meaning "and any one to whom the Son reveals these things."

As a matter of fact, I cast my ballot against Winter's logic, with many expressions of appreciation for the superb job he has done of gathering the evidence. I cannot convince myself that the questioned clause should be omitted. And,

---

34. *Novum Testamentum*, 1 (1956), 131.
35. *Novum Testamentum*, 1 (1956), 143.

although it would offer certain obvious advantages to my own understanding of the passage, I do not really believe in the alternative I have proposed above (namely, that the implied object of ἀποκαλύψαι is "these things"). The evidence bearing on the order in Matthew is not fully convincing in either direction. The early patristic order is the more difficult. On the other hand, the early Fathers may have reversed the sequence in *memoriter* citing because the knowledge of the Father is the greater mystery. In my opinion, on either order, the last clause really means "and any one to whom the Son reveals him." It is *not* logical. But it is true to the experience of a community to whom the Son *had* revealed the Father—a community, by the way, which also confessed that its knowledge of the Son was revealed *by* the Father as well (Matt. 16:17).

Matt. 11:25–27 and Matt. 11:28–30

Our further treatment of the section Matt. 11:25–27 requires that we consider whether verses 28–30 have been added by Matthew to the Q-sayings in verses 25–27 or whether that connection was already made in Q. There are weighty arguments in favor of the position that the connection was first made by Matthew. However, since the appearance of E. Norden's *Agnostos Theos*,[36] considerable support has been given to the idea that the whole of Matt. 11:25–30 constitutes a traditional unity. Norden regarded the section as an example of a kind of missionary propaganda widely characteristic of the Hellenistic world. It is, he thought, a three-strophe hymn based on a pattern of "self-recommendation" in Gnostic circles. The continued acceptance of this basic proposal may be indicated by K. Stendahl's comment on the passage in the recent *Peake's Commentary*:

The hymnic character of these verses is recognized with precision since Eduard Norden . . . drew attention to a pattern of such "self-revelation": (a) Thanksgiving to the Father for received revelation; (b) statement of its content; (c) invitation and appeal. This

---

36. E. Norden, *Agnostos Theos*, (Stuttgart: Teubner, 1956), pp. 277–311.

structure gives Matthew's form as the complete one priority over the Lucan form (only a and b).[37]

Norden found evidence of his *Redetypus* in such diverse sources as the *Poimandres*, the Odes of Solomon, and Sirach.

In 1935, Norden's analysis was given a fresh turn by Martin Rist, who wrote:

It has been shown that the Hermetic hymns of rebirth and the charge of the Isiac priest to the initiate, which bear such striking resemblance to the phraseology of the gospel pericope, reflect the experience of initiation into the cult. To follow this suggestion, if the gospel passage, with its strophic division, rhythmic movement, and mystical thought, be considered a liturgical hymn used in connection with the rite of Christian baptism, its difficulties of interpretation are largely dissolved.[38]

That the pericope was capable of being put to such use was demonstrated by Rist with reference to Clement of Alexandria.

Two years later, Tomas Arvedson published his *Das Mysterium Christi*, a full monograph treatment of our passage, which likewise took Norden's three-strophe hymn as its beginning point. Arvedson regarded the pattern as cultic in origin and attempted to trace its features in material separated by such temporal and spatial distance as ancient Near Eastern royal inscriptions, the Hebrew thanksgiving ritual, and the Isiac mysteries. He concluded that "the pericope Matt. 11:25–30 is a liturgy, originally appointed for a mystery ceremony whose center was the enthronement of Christ."[39] All three studies are very suggestive and the very fact that verses 25–26 constitute a prayer makes the proposal of a liturgical *Sitz im Leben* natural.[40]

---

37. *Peake's Commentary*, p. 784.
38. Martin Rist, "Is Matt. 11:25–30 a Primitive Baptismal Hymn?" *Journal of Religion*, 15 (January 1935), 73.
39. *Das Mysterium Christi*, p. 229.
40. Heinz Becker, *Die Reden des Johannesevangeliums und der Stil der gnostischen Offenbarungsrede*, Forschungen zur Religion und Literatur des Alten und Neuen Testaments 68 (Göttingen: Vandenhoeck and Ruprecht, 1956), describes a

These theories, however, require that the whole of Matt. 11:25–30 be a pre-Matthean unity determined by a pattern which can be paralleled outside the church, and there are decisive reasons why the section cannot be regarded as a unity of this kind:

(1) The absence of verses 28–30 from the Lucan parallel (10:21–22) is, to be sure, an argument from silence. However, if the saying had been found in Q at this point, it is difficult to understand why Luke would have omitted it. Moreover, it is sometimes overlooked that Luke 10:23–24 preserves, immediately after the logion concerning the knowledge of the Father and the Son, a saying which—from the point of view of *content*—is thoroughly appropriate to the Q-context. This is the familiar saying which begins, "Blessed are the eyes which see what you see!" Matthew also preserves this beatitude; but he has removed it to a Markan context (13: 16–17).

(2) Some weight must be given to Bultmann's contention that Matt. 11:27 and 11:28–30 are very different, since "v. 27 promises revelation" while "in vv. 28–30 the teacher makes his appeal and promises a reward for obeying his commands."[41] Bultmann regards the former as a Hellenistic revelation saying and the latter as a quotation from Jewish Wisdom tradition. In fact, both sayings are probably derived

revelation discourse form consisting of three parts: (1) Self-predication, (2) Invitation, and (3) *Krisenspruch* (Promise and/or Threat). Matt. 11:28–30, which is characterized by the invitation in the imperative and the promise in the future, may be related to parts (2) and (3) of Becker's discourse. However, Matt. 11:25–27 is still left unexplained, since (a) the evidence indicates that they were originally independent of verses 28–30, (b) the form of the invitation would require Sophia rather than the Son as the subject of (1), and (c) Becker's pattern does not explain verses 25–26 at all.

However, Becker's study is very important for a discussion of "The Scheme of the Revelation Discourse in Proverbs and Sirach" (pp. 41–53). He finds the three motifs mentioned above in Proverbs 8 and Sirach 24, and he discusses a related form—shaped by prophetic discourse—in Proverbs 1. The wisdom material, he indicates, makes clear the antiquity of the pattern which he says has a pre-Gnostic and predualistic stage, although it "was actually predisposed for utilization as a *Krisis*-pattern of the Gnostic revealer" (p. 53).

The recognition of a predualistic and pre-Gnostic stage of the pattern is significant for the interpretation of 11:28–30.

41. *History of the Synoptic Tradition*, p. 159.

from Wisdom tradition, but in that tradition a distinction between the Son and Sophia is maintained which Matthew's arrangement obliterates.

(3) Verses 28–30 appear in the Gospel of Thomas (saying 90) independent of the thanksgiving and revelation strophes.

(4) Most important, the cornerstone of the structure, when 11:25–30 is treated as a unit, is the parallel with Sirach 51. Arvedson states that his investigation begins from the presupposition that the similarities between Sirach and Matthew "cannot be accidental."[42] While Norden lists numerous parallels to the form of the supposed hymn, Sirach 51 is the most convincing. The second best is perhaps that in the *Poimandres*, but the pattern in that work is a bit abnormal and would be quite hard to find without Matthew and Sirach as pointers. In short, Sirach 51 is the link between Matthew and the remainder of the material. Especially for Norden and Arvedson, the relation between these two must be other than merely literary; that is, both Sirach and Matthew must be shown to be variant forms of the same pattern of proclamation or liturgy. That they are related in this way is not demonstrated beyond doubt by Norden and Arvedson. Now, the discovery of 11 QPs[a] makes it all but impossible, for this Qumran Davidic psalter contains an older form of the Wisdom hymn found in Sirach 51:13–30. The significance of this find is three-fold: (a) It demonstrates clearly that the author of Sir. 51:13–30 was not Jeshua ben Sira. (b) This in turn requires a purely literary, rather than liturgical-traditional, relation of this song to the Thanksgiving hymn in Sir. 51:1–12. The literary relation probably should have been clear enough already from the fact that the two portions of the chapter are in very different styles.[43]

42. *Das Mysterium Christi*, p. 8.

43. *Cf.* James M. Robinson, "Die Hodajot-Formel in Gebet und Hymnus des Frühchristentums," in *Apophoreta: Festschrift für Ernst Haenchen*, ed. W. Eltester and F. H. Kettler (Berlin: Alfred Töpelmann, 1964), p. 227, n. 63 (hereafter cited as "Hodajot-Formel"). Of course, the Amidah-like prayer found between verses 12 and 13 of the Hebrew text already pointed to the composite character of Sirach 51.

Hans Dieter Betz, "The Logion of the Easy Yoke and of Rest," *Journal of Biblical Literature*, 86 (September 1967), 10–24, also rejects the unity of Matt. 11:25–30. Betz provides a convenient summary of the most important critical discussion. Behind Matt. 11:28–30 and similar sayings in later Gnostic documents he postu-

(c) It shows that some elements which Arvedson treated as "cultic" in the song are secondary and are probably due to a bowdlerizing of its original erotic language.[44]

For these reasons, we must suppose that verses 28–30 did not stand in Q but were interpolated by Matthew. This does not mean, however, that a search for a liturgical setting for verses 25–27 is wholly inappropriate. James Robinson has recently discussed this passage quite briefly in a long study of "The Hodayoth Formula in Early Christian Prayer and Hymn."[45] The formal similarity between the words, "I thank thee Father, Lord of heaven and earth, that thou hast hidden these things from the wise and understanding and revealed them to babes," and the introductory formulas of the Qumran Thanksgiving hymns is clear. Robinson traces the long history of the formula in prayers of sectarian Judaism and early Christianity; he regards the Hodayoth as—at least in part—a polemically motivated alternative to the normal Jewish Berakoth.[46] An important section of the article establishes a close link between ecstatic prayers and hymns in early Christian prophecy.[47] He regards Matt. 11:25–27 as an example of such an inspired thanksgiving which has been kept "in all purity."[48] Robinson appears to favor giving

---

lates originally independent wisdom sayings "which were gnosticized and then were taken up in different variants into the Gospel of Matthew, the Gospel of Thomas, and the Pistis Sophia" (p. 20).

44. *E.g.*, Arvedson, *Das Mysterium Christi*, p. 83, n. 4, says that "two sentences of the LXX-text, which have no clear counterpart in our Hebrew text, have a decided sacral ring, namely, 14a . . . and 19c." But 11 QPs* now shows that 14a in LXX is a pious toning-down of the original. And, while 19c is partially defective in the Qumran manuscript, the LXX is probably not true to the original in this verse either. *Cf.* J. A. Sanders, *The Psalms Scroll of Qumran Cave 11*, Discoveries in the Judean Desert of Jordan 4 (Oxford: Clarendon, 1965), p. 80, for a convenient arrangement of LXX and 11 QPs* texts in parallel columns.

45. See n. 43 above.

46. J. P. Audet, "Literary Forms and Contents of a Normal Εὐχαριστία in the First Century," *Studia Evangelica, Texte und Untersuchungen* 73 (Berlin: Akademie, 1959), 643–662 regards our passage as an example of a "spontaneous" (as opposed to "cultual") benediction of two parts (p. 648) modeled on "the Jewish 'benediction' (berâkhâh) which has been . . . the true parent of the Christian εὐχαριστία . . ." (p. 646). See also Audet, "Esquisse Historique du Genre Littéraire de la 'Bénédiction' Juive et de l'' Eucharistie' Chrétienne," *Revue Biblique*, 65 (July 1958), 371–399.

47. "Hodajot-Formel," pp. 221–226.

48. "Hodajot-Formel," p. 226.

this mode of expression its primary setting in the Eucharist (*the* Thanksgiving), a setting whose appropriateness is most quickly seen in the prayer of Did. 10:2–5.

However, if Robinson's analysis of 1 Cor. 12–14 is correct, this limitation is probably narrower than the form itself requires; as a part of pneumatic worship, it might be found in various liturgical settings. Moreover, Robinson also recognizes that the formula has "a non-liturgical background embedded in everyday speech," which has strongly affected one type of Pauline epistolary thanksgiving.[49] Even from the point of view of content, for example, the thanksgiving section of 1 Corinthians (1:4–7) has striking affinities with our passage: "I give thanks to God always for you because of the grace of God which was given you in Christ Jesus, that in every way you were enriched in him with all speech and knowledge . . . so that you are not lacking in any spiritual gift, as you wait for the revealing of our Lord Jesus Christ."

Thus, I am inclined to doubt that considerations of form in themselves are sufficient to define the specific setting to which the saying in Matt. 11:25–27 belongs. There is the additional matter of content which must be pondered. This provides for us a kind of dilemma similar to that posed by the Qumran thanksgiving hymns; our passage is like those hymns in that, as Millar Burrows has pointed out, "the most distinctive individual element is the consciousness of having received a divine revelation."[50] Considerations of neither form nor content have permitted a specific definition of the *Sitz im Leben* of the thanksgiving hymns. The problem is that our knowledge of the worship life of Qumran is too limited and the potentialities for the use of the hymns too broad to permit assured conclusions. With respect to our passage, it appears to me that the hymn in Matthew 11 may be assigned to any setting in worship where thanksgiving for revelation is appropriate. On the basis of our present knowledge of worship in the New Testament period, the most obvious

---

49. "Hodajot-Formel," p. 201.

50. Millar Burrows, *More Light on the Dead Sea Scrolls* (New York: Viking, 1958), p. 381.

settings would be the Eucharist, as Robinson has suggested, or Baptism, as Rist suggested on other grounds.

It is interesting to note that 1 Corinthians 1–2 is almost universally recognized as furnishing instructive parallels to this passage. Because Paul's whole discussion of the "wise of this world," the revelation to "babes" and to "the mature," and so on, has as at least its point of departure the issue of baptism, this may provide a more fitting setting than the Eucharist. In fact, the designation of the recipients of the revelation as "babes" may in itself point in this direction. The setting would be particularly attractive if we could feel confidence in the judgment of A. M. Hunter's "scientific guess" and place the saying following a confession of faith.[51]

The Revelation to Babes

The prayer shows every sign of having been derived from a type of Jewish wisdom thought which has passed through an apocalyptic medium. It is sometimes assumed that a "revelation to babes rather than to the wise" runs directly against the current of Jewish thought. And, if 4 Ezra were taken as the model, then such would appear to be the case. Revelation of the eschatological mysteries is there—as elsewhere in Jewish literature—reserved for the elect:

But think of your own case, and inquire concerning the glory of those who are like yourself, because it is for you that paradise is opened . . . the age to come is prepared . . . rest is appointed . . . and wisdom perfected beforehand . . . Therefore, my judgment is now drawing near; I have not shown this to all men, but only to you and a few like you (4 Ezra 8:51–52, 61–62).

Q has given our hymn an eschatological setting by placing it in immediate proximity to the woes on the Galilean cities. Yet, "these things" in Q are said to be "hidden from the wise and revealed to babes." And on the surface, this appears to be very different from what is found subsequently in 4 Ezra.

51. A. M. Hunter, "Crux Criticorum—Mt. xi. 25–30—a Re-appraisal," *New Testament Studies*, 8 (1961–62), 243. Hunter, however, is pursuing a setting in the life of Jesus for the logion, a pursuit that I would regard as a lost cause even if the saying is genuine.

For example, at 4 Ezra 12:35–38 the seer is told:

This is the dream that you saw, and this is its interpretation. And you alone were worthy to learn this secret of the Most High. Therefore write all these things that you have seen in a book, and put it in a hidden place; and you shall teach them to the wise among your people, whose hearts you know are able to comprehend and keep these secrets.

In 4 Ezra 14:40–47, wisdom is again "hidden" in written books. The revelation of the contents of the ninety-four books is a function of one who has understanding and wisdom. The secret character of the revelation is emphasized by the "unknown alphabet" in which the amanuensis is instructed to write. The twenty-four books are for public reading, but the seventy are reserved for the eyes of the wise. "For in them is the spring of understanding, the fountain of wisdom and the river of knowledge" (verse 47).

Now, to the degree that the "wise" in 4 Ezra are the "scribes" or "men of understanding," these passages do stand in contradiction to the revelation to "babes." But this overlooks the fact that in Jewish usage the "wise man" is also the good, the pious, the man who trusts in God. The "wise" of 4 Ezra and the "babes" of the Q saying are, in fact, the "elect" under different titles. The denial of wisdom to the "wise of the world" and its revelation to the "humble" is not something new in the Wisdom stream; indeed, it is almost a dogma of late Jewish wisdom, as Hahn correctly sees.[52] It appears in the distinction between the mighty ones and the elect ones of both 1 Enoch and Wisdom of Solomon. It also appears, in a form dependent on the old pattern of the inaccessibility of Wisdom, in Baruch 3, where it is said that Wisdom is not known to such legendary wise men as those who dwell in Canaan and Teman, as the "sons of Hagar who seek for understanding on the earth, the merchants of Merran and Teman, the story-tellers and the seekers for

52. Ferdinand Hahn, *Christologische Hoheitstitel*, Forschungen zur Religion und Literatur des Alten und Neuen Testaments 83, (Göttingen: Vandenhoeck and Ruprecht, 1963), p. 322.

understanding," none of whom "have learned the way to wisdom" (3:21–23); yet Wisdom is given to the elect—that is, to Israel. It is customary to cite 1 Cor. 1:18–20 in connection with our passage, because of the way it speaks of God having made "foolish the wisdom of the world," which according to Paul belongs to the "wise man" and the "debater of this age." But the antiquity of the idea of the rejection of the "wise in the ways of worldly wisdom" is shown by the fact that Paul's argument rides along on the crest of a quotation from Is. 29:14, "I will destroy the wisdom of the wise, and the cleverness of the clever I will thwart." Proverbial wisdom already knew that "there is more hope for a fool" than for "a man who is wise in his own eyes" (Prov. 26:12). Job taught about the wise who do not see (Job 15:2, LXX). Thus, in 1 Enoch 5:8, the eschatological reward of the righteous is described like this:

> And then there shall be bestowed upon the elect wisdom,
> And they shall all live and never again sin,
> Either through ungodliness or through pride:
> But they who are wise shall be humble.

Perhaps the closest parallel to our passage is found in the Qumran Manual of Discipline 11:6–7, which W. H. Brownlee translated:

> My eye has beheld that wisdom
> Which was hidden from men of knowledge,
> And that prudent purpose [which was hidden] from the sons
> of men:
> A fountain of righteousness and reservoir of strength
> As well as a spring of glory [which were concealed] from the
> assembly of flesh.[53]

The sources of the contrast between the mighty and the humble, the wise and the innocent, are actually quite complex: the ideal of humility in ancient wisdom, the pessimism

53. W. H. Brownlee, tr., *The Dead Sea Manual of Discipline*, Bulletin of the American Schools of Oriental Research, Supplementary Studies 10–12 (New Haven: American Schools of Oriental Research, 1951).

of sceptical wisdom, the essentially eschatological distinction between the unrighteous great and the pious humble, and the prophetic opposition of revelation to worldly wisdom. This is what stands behind the "wise men and babes" of Matt. 11:25–26. And it is also the background, not only of 1 Cor. 1:18–21, but also of 1 Cor. 1:26–29:

For consider your call, brethren: not many of you were wise according to worldly standards, not many were powerful, not many were of noble birth; but God chose what is foolish in the world to shame the wise, God chose what is weak in the world to shame the strong, God chose what is low and despised in the world, even things that are not, to bring to nothing things that are, so that no human being might boast in the presence of God.

Whether one speaks of how it "pleased" God to reveal these things to babes or of God's choice of that which is foolish and lowly, one speaks of the action of God in relation to the elect. It is no wonder that Harnack said, "Whenever I read 1 Cor. i. 19, 21 . . . I am ever again struck by the coincidence here, both in thought and vocabulary, with [Matt. 11:25–26], though all of course has been passed through the crucible" of Paul's mind.[54]

If, as Harnack thought and I believe likely, this hymn was known to Paul (in fact, was in the apostle's mind) as he wrote 1 Corinthians, it is striking that the apostle speaks of "a secret and hidden wisdom of God" which is imparted to the mature (τέλειοι) but *not* to those who are "babes" (1 Cor. 2:6—3:3). Is it possible that "babes" in Corinth had become a title of pride, rather than a badge of humility? Because they have turned the "wisdom of God" into a "wisdom of their own," these "babes" were really only "fleshly beings" (3:3), not yet "spiritual" (2:14)—and thus could not understand the wisdom which Paul imparted to the "mature."

It is clear, at any rate, that thanksgiving is offered in our passage for a revelation vouchsafed only to the "elect," who

---

54. *The Sayings of Jesus*, p. 301; also cited in Hunter, *New Testament Studies*, 8 (1961–62), 244.

are designated "babes," while the "wise" are regarded as being outside the circle of election.

The chief remaining question in verses 25–26 is what "these things" are which are said to be revealed. If the hymn has found a setting in Q totally foreign to the setting which it had in Christian worship, then perhaps the most that we can say is that "these things" obviously has reference to the saving revelation given the community, which from verse 27 we assume would consist essentially of the revelation of the Father which comes only through the Son. However, the fact that the hymn was found in Q in close relation to the "Woes on the Galilean cities" (Matt. 11:20–24) has led to two efforts to become more specific about the nature and content of the revelation.

"These Things" Are Revealed

The relation of the hymn to the woes was part of the evidence on the basis of which Arvedson argued for a mystery liturgy as the hymn's *Sitz im Leben*. Arvedson understood the woes in terms of formulas of inclusion and exclusion in initiation ceremonies, with antecedents in the cultic blessings and curses delineated by Sigmund Mowinckel in such passages as Deuteronomy 27–28 and 11:13–21.[55] In addition to the warnings spoken by the κῆρυξ in Hellenistic initiation ceremonies, one thinks immediately also of the formulas used by the "men of the covenant" at Qumran. There is a great deal to be said in favor of some such suggestion. For example, the woes against the Pharisees and scribes followed by Wisdom's oracle of doom in Matthew 23 might be considered a partial parallel. On this same analogy, the Matthean form of the Beatitudes is followed by an "I-have-come" saying and perhaps could be treated as "words of inclusion."[56] But it is doubtful that these obviously Matthean constructs can be used to prove anything about the traditional setting for the hymn. Moreover, while beatitudes and woes are found

55. Sigmund Mowinckel, *Psalmenstudien* (Amsterdam: P. Schippers, 1961), 5: 75–80, 101–107.

56. Hans Windisch, *The Meaning of the Sermon on the Mount*, tr. S. M. Gilmour (Philadelphia: Westminster, 1951), pp. 27–29.

side by side in Luke's Sermon on the Plain, there is nothing in the context to encourage a liturgical understanding of them; similarly, Luke's woes against the scribes and lawyers are not so organized as to encourage such an interpretation, and at the crucial spot (Luke 11:45–52) I would regard Luke's order as closer to Q. In the passage we are considering, the intrusion of Luke 10:17–20 between the woes against the Galilean cities and the hymn raises a question as to how closely the two were related in Q.[57] It is possible that Arvedson has provided us with a valuable hint here. I would feel more confidence in trying to pursue the clue at this point, if I had sufficient reasons for assuming that Matthew's context is that of Q. In other places (Matt. 16:17–19; 5:11–16) Matthew has preserved and/or constructed material to fit the pattern of a commissioning "liturgy." Here, however, it seems to me that Matthew has sacrificed whatever liturgical setting the hymn might have had for another purpose which we will examine later. It is with some reluctance that Arvedson's proposal (even in a considerably modified form) has been set aside as improbable.

W. D. Davies has argued that the woes require an eschatological interpretation of "these things" in verse 25.[58] And, if either Matthew or Luke has preserved Q's order, it is difficult to quarrel with this conclusion. Q shares the eschatological expectation of the early church, and for it "these things" probably has to do with the revelation of the approaching end, its signs (which, for Q, are no clearly discernible signs), and its heralds. The eschatological thrust of the hymn is also to be seen by the pericope which follows it in Luke 10:23–24: "Then turning to the disciples he said privately, 'Blessed are the eyes which see what you see! For I tell you that many prophets and kings desired to see what you see, and did not see it, and to hear what you hear, and

---

57. Arvedson's attempt (*Das Mysterium Christi*, pp. 112–114, 128–130) to relate the whole mission of the disciples to the hymn as a reflection of his hypothetical liturgy seems most improbable. He appeals to the association of revelation and commissioning in Hellenistic mysteries, but the examples he cites would lead us to expect the thanksgiving to precede the commission and the mission.

58. W. D. Davies, "'Knowledge' in the Dead Sea Scrolls and in Matthew 11: 25–30," *Harvard Theological Review*, 46 (July 1953), 137–138.

did not hear it.'" Thus, the "these things" in verse 25 should be understood as referring to eschatological secrets.

The Son

The saying which is joined to the thanksgiving in Q (Matt. 11:27, Luke 10:22) has occasioned considerable debate concerning the background against which it is to be understood. Bultmann considers it "an Hellenistic Revelation saying, as Dibelius has rightly characterized it."[59] He cites as a *religionsgeschichtlich* parallel the lines, "No other knows thee save Thy Son, Akhnaton. Thou hast initiated him into thy plans and thy powers," from Akhnaton's Hymn to the Sun. As an extreme example of where this interpretation may lead, we may cite Arvedson's comment:

If our interpretation is correct, that means that the outlook of the saying *is typically Gnostic* . . . The verse could have stood in any appropriate syncretistic text just as well as in Matthew's Gospel. From the perspective of this passage, it is therefore simply impossible to establish any distinction in the outlook, a most noteworthy witness to how great the agreement between the New Testament— in this case the Logia source—and syncretism is.[60]

The opposing view has been stated with polemic sharpness by A. M. Hunter, who does not think it is permissible

to dismiss the saying blandly as a Hellenistic 'revelation word'. The Hellenistic parallels to it (like the hymn to Echnaton) raked up by Reitzenstein and Co., were never impressive, and in the last two decades the discovery of the Dead Sea Scrolls has altered the whole picture . . . Not Hellenism but Hosea (a book well-known to Jesus)—not pagan *gnosis* but O. T. *da'ath Elohim*—supplies the likeliest background to the supreme "I-Thou" relationship of Matt. xi. 27.[61]

Now it does not appear to me that the views advanced by the extreme representatives of either of these positions is

59. *History of the Synoptic Tradition*, p. 160.
60. *Das Mysterium Christi*, pp. 154–155.
61. *New Testament Studies*, 8 (1961–62), 245.

likely to be correct. On the one hand, a Hellenistic revelation saying is—after all—a form that is Oriental in origin. It should not be a matter of surprise if such a form were to appear in a Jewish writing. "Hellenistic" simply does not mean "non-Jewish." As Helmut H. Koester exclaims, "As if Judaism itself were not already a product of Oriental syncretism! And as if even the Christian-gnostic writings of the second century did not have such deep roots in Jewish theology!"[62] On the other hand, the processes of cultural adaptation, accommodation, and assimilation characteristic of the Hellenistic period should never be read in such a way that local distinctiveness is obscured. Formal parallels between material found in a Jewish setting and material found in (for example) an Hermetic saying does not always imply identity of meaning. W. D. Davies goes too far perhaps in speaking of a Judaism which "had been invaded by Hellenistic terminology" but which "had not . . . modified its essential nature."[63] But it is dangerous to allow formal and terminological parallels to carry more weight than they can bear in a sociologically ambiguous situation.

I think that the way out of the interpretative dilemma posed by verse 27 has been pointed by Davies in his well-known essay on "'Knowledge' in the Dead Sea Scrolls and Matthew 11:25–30."[64] Davies assumes that Matt. 11:25–27 constitutes a unit, an assumption which I regard as valid. The problem, therefore, becomes one of dealing with the two parts of the hymn—the thanksgiving, in which knowledge of eschatological secrets is implied, and the revelation word, in which an "intimate knowledge of the Father" is spoken of. Davies convincingly marshals evidence from the Dead Sea materials to show that at Qumran such a juxtaposition of eschatological and intimate knowledge is to be found. Thus, a Jewish background for understanding the saying is proposed. I think Davies is too cautious in his restriction of the

62. Helmut H. Koester, "Häretiker in Urchristentums als theologisches Problem," *Zeit und Geschichte*, ed. E. Dinkler (Tübingen: J. C. B. Mohr [Paul Siebeck], 1964), p. 65. Koester is discussing the criteria for determining heresy in the early church and the modern tendency to regard "Jewish" ideas as "orthodox."

63. *Harvard Theological Review*, 46 (1953), 139.

64. *Harvard Theological Review*, 46 (1953), 133–139.

degree of "Hellenistic" influence, but this is in part a result of his definition of "Hellenism." And it is plain that the Old Testament by itself cannot explain our passage or the Qumran parallels for Davies, since he writes:

Nevertheless, one thing is observable when we seek to understand the circles in which the DSS emerged. They seem to have placed a greater emphasis upon the concept of knowledge, whatever its exact connotation, than the more strictly Jewish circles, whose literature across the centuries is preserved in the Old Testament. This may well be due to the influence of Hellenistic factors.[65]

In my opinion, the wisdom stream is to be viewed as the locus of this special concern with knowledge. And, for the interpretation of our verse, it seems to me to be necessary to move in the direction Davies points but beyond the Qumran material for understanding. The most illuminating parallels are to be found in the Wisdom of Solomon, a writing with many features that are reminiscent of the Dead Sea documents.

B. W. Bacon argued as long ago as 1916 that the Matthean hymn is the product of "lyric wisdom" and that the language concerning the mutual knowledge of the Son and the Father has roots in "the idea of Israel as the People of Revelation."[66] The key "is the pre-Christian doctrine of Election—the Chosen People as the divine Organ of Revelation,"[67] of which the figure of the servant in Deutero-Isaiah is the supreme example.

The clearest instance of the way in which this idea becomes focused on a single individual is to be found in the Wisdom of Solomon, which speaks of one who "professes to have knowledge of God, and calls himself a *child* of the Lord . . . and boasts that God is his *father*" (2:13, 16). About him, his adversaries say:

65. *Harvard Theological Review*, 46 (1953), 135.
66. B. W. Bacon, "The 'Son' as Organ of Revelation," *Harvard Theological Review*, 9 (October 1916), 382–415, esp. p. 385.
67. *Harvard Theological Review*, 9 (1916), 415.

Let us see if his words are true,
and let us test what will happen at the end of his life;
for if the righteous man is *God's son*, he will help him. (2:17-18)[68]

The reasoning of the adversaries is said to be wrong because "they did not know the secret purposes (μυστήρια) of God" (2:22). In a passage that may have originally been applied to Enoch[69] and interpolated into the description of this Son of God, it is said:

There was one who pleased God and was loved by him,
and while living among sinners he was taken up . . .
Being perfected in a short time, he fulfilled long years;
for his soul was pleasing to the Lord,
therefore he took him quickly from the midst of wickedness.
Yet the peoples saw and did not understand,
nor take such a thing to heart,
that God's grace and mercy are with his elect,
and he watches over his holy ones. (4:10, 13-15)

Moreover, in a judgment scene of near-apocalyptic intensity, this Son stands fully vindicated before his opponents, before whom he now serves as a revelation of God's purposes (see especially 4:20—5:16).

Thus, the Wisdom of Solomon furnishes the background against which the revealed knowledge in Matt. 11:25–27 can be seen in its relation to election, to eschatological knowledge, to the intimate relation of Father and Son, and the failure of men to know the Son as well as the Father.

68. It is true, as I showed in my article, "Wisdom of Solomon 2:10—5:A Homily Based on the Fourth Servant Song," *Journal of Biblical Literature*, 76 (March 1959), 26–33, that the title "Son" in these passages is a result of the author's misunderstanding of the term παῖς in the LXX Servant Songs of Deutero-Isaiah. However, that does not affect the applicability of these passages, for the author of the Wisdom of Solomon certainly knew what the alternative meanings for παῖς were. The fact that he understood παῖς as equivalent to υἱός only shows that his theological milieu had already supplied "Son" as a title for one like the Servant. Marc Philonenko, "Le Maître de justice et la Sagesse de Solomon," *Theologische Zeitschrift*, 14 (1958), 81–88, apparently believes that "Solomon" used παῖς to mean Servant and υἱός to mean Son. If Philonenko is correct, then my point is made more clearly, but I doubt that he is right.

69. See above, Chapter One, n. 41.

About the Son in Wisdom of Solomon, this further must be said. He is a typical figure, and it is clear at points that he is to some degree representative of the people. Who has been chosen to sit for the portrait of this typical figure? It is not enough to say that he is modeled on the Servant of Deutero-Isaiah. For to "Solomon" the Servant was a σοφός (4:17) who—like all of Wisdom's children—was rejected by his contemporaries. To say that he is a σοφός, a wise man, at all is to imply the function of teacher. But to speak of a wise man in the context of the Wisdom of Solomon is to speak of one whom Sophia has made "a friend of God," who has "learned both what is secret and what is manifest, for wisdom, the fashioner of all things, taught [him]" (6:21-22).

The rejection of this prophetic figure does not seem to be a prominent feature of the New Testament hymn, where it is encapsulated in the clause, "No one knows the Son except the Father." So brief a description of the rejection of the prophet is surprising in view of the lengthy recital of affliction in the forms which have been suggested as the source of the pattern of our hymn—whether it be the Thanksgiving Psalms of the canon or the Hodayoth of Qumran. But it would be a serious mistake to regard the afflictions of the Qumran psalmist(s) and those of the righteous Son in the Wisdom of Solomon as being redemptive for others or even as being a part of the revelation the prophets mediate. Affliction is a conventional, circumstantial component of the career through which the righteous man is borne along by the confidence that he will be vindicated, and his vindication guarantees, not the redemptive significance of his death, but the truth of his teaching. M. Philonenko rejects this view of the suffering of the Son in the Wisdom of Solomon because it "borders on docetism."[70] But, as Dieter Georgi has shown, the typical character of the understanding of history and the specific descriptions of the Righteous One in the Wisdom of Solomon do border on docetism.[71] (Cf. Wisd. of Sol. 3:1-3: "But the souls of the righteous are in the hand of God, and

70. *Theologische Zeitschrift*, 14 (1958), 86.

71. Dieter Georgi, "Der vorpaulinische Hymnus in Phil. 2, 6–11," in *Zeit und Geschichte*, pp. 272–275.

no torment will ever touch them. In the eyes of the foolish they seemed to have died . . . but they are at peace.") The Son of our hymn—like the Son of the Wisdom of Solomon—is "not known" to men; that is, he is rejected. The rejection has its place as a part of the expected career, but it in no way affects the fact that the Son functions primarily as the mediator of revelation.

Thus, Tödt properly describes the community in which the Q tradition had its home as one which did not understand the passion and resurrection as something which "had to be preached."

They wanted to go on preaching what Jesus had preached. But what had this to do with the passion and resurrection? As understood by this community, the passion and resurrection were not what had to be preached but what had enabled them to preach. The events of Jesus' being executed, laid under the curse of the cross and turned out of Israel could not fail to cast doubt upon the authority of his teaching. . . .

However, "what happened after the resurrection must have been understood as the Lord's turning anew in love towards his own.". . .

Seeing the resurrection thus, a community which was deeply sure of the resurrection nevertheless might follow its commission in another way than by primarily preaching passion and resurrection; for their view the gift of salvation did not lie in these events, but had been validated by them.[72]

This understanding of the situation in the community which pronounced Q is developed by Tödt in a study which concentrates its attention on the Son of man aspect of the tradition. In view of what we have seen above about the relation of the Son of man to Wisdom, it should not be surprising to us that an examination of passages in which Jesus is regarded

72. Tödt, *The Son of Man in the Synoptic Tradition*, tr. D. M. Barton (Philadelphia: Westminster, 1965), pp. 250–251.

as the representative of Sophia should point in the same direction.[73]

The Q hymn thus opens with thanksgiving for the eschatological secrets given to the elect; it speaks of the revelation entrusted to the Son who is not known by men, and—even if paradoxically—of that Son's revelation of the Father to his followers. This picture of the Son is derived from the world of thought represented by the Wisdom of Solomon, although now the righteous and wise man is viewed as a concrete historical (rather than typical) figure who serves as the organ of revelation.

The Thanksgiving-Revelation Unit in Matthew

What Matthew has done to this hymn may be shown in almost summary fashion. First of all, his arrangement of the text has effected a modification in the significance of "these things" which have "been revealed to babes" in verse 25. The reference is still to the "mighty works" as eschatological signs mentioned in the woes against the Galilean cities but these mighty works are interpreted by Matthew, as we have seen, by the preceding section as the "deeds of the Christ" which are nothing else than the "deeds of incarnate Wisdom."[74]

Matthew's second alteration is the addition of the saying about "the light yoke" in verses 28–30. There does not seem to be anyone to question that this saying is dependent on

73. Thus, what Edward P. Blair says of Matt. 11:27-30 is accurate with respect to Q: "The Gospel of Matthew as a whole is simply a commentary on the crucially important passage 11:27-30. The Father has revealed his secrets to the Son. The Son in turn reveals them to his disciples. He thus invites men to come and learn from him, and if they do, they will find rest for their souls. The Son is the World's teacher and savior (28:18-20). Upon their comprehension of his teaching their salvation rests" (*Jesus in the Gospel of Matthew* [New York: Abingdon, 1960], p. 108). This statement by itself is less adequate for Matthew than for Q, however. As Blair recognizes, Jesus is not in Matthew simply the teacher. By bringing Q into the framework of a gospel, Matthew has given the passion and resurrection too large a place for Jesus to be conceived in this fashion only. (Verses 28–30 were not in Q.)

74. W. D. Davies, *The Setting of the Sermon on the Mount* (Cambridge, England: Cambridge University Press, 1964), p. 207, mentions the reference back to "the deeds of Christ."

Jewish Wisdom literature. Customarily, reference is made to Sir. 51 : 26–27, where the author declares:

> Put your neck under the yoke,
> and let your souls receive instruction;
> it is to be found close by.
> See with your eyes that I have labored little
> and found for myself much rest.

Sirach 6 also speaks of "putting your neck into her collar," (verse 24), of "coming to her with all your soul" (verse 26), of her yoke as a "golden ornament" (verse 30), and of the "rest which she gives" (verse 28).

However, in all these passages, it is never a matter of the σοφός inviting men to take the yoke of the teacher—rather he counsels men to accept the yoke of Wisdom. Here, however, we observe again how Matthew has placed on the lips of Jesus a saying appropriate only to Wisdom, not to Wisdom's representative. Just as in Matt. 23:34–36 Jesus, as incarnate Wisdom, can speak Sophia's oracle of doom, just as in Matt. 23:37–39 he can, in the same role, utter Wisdom's lament, so, in this place, Jesus issues Wisdom's call. His ἐγώ and the ἐγώ of Sophia are one. R. M. Grant is, therefore, correct when he writes, "But in this passage in Matthew we do not hear about Wisdom from Jesus son of Sirach; we hear the words of Jesus the Wisdom of God."[75] Matthew has once again moved beyond Q, for which Jesus as the Son is the mediator of revelation, the idealized σοφός; now the Son is identified with Wisdom. Once again we have to observe that this fateful step of identifying Jesus with Sophia made by Paul at Corinth and by Matthew (in Syria?) is a development which was required before the gnosticising tendencies of their opponents could issue in the developed Gnosticism of the second century. To quote Grant in relation to Matt. 11: 28–30 again, "There is a Wisdom-Christology in this passage which points toward the Gnostic speculations about Wisdom."[76]

75. R. M. Grant, *Gnosticism and Early Christianity* (New York: Columbia University Press, 1959), p. 153.
76. *Gnosticism and Early Christianity*, p. 153.

With the introduction of Wisdom's invitation, the study of Wisdom motifs in Matthew turns in a new direction which we will delineate in the final chapter. I hope that our investigation thus far has served to establish that speculation about Wisdom emanated from circles which tended to see Jesus' significance largely in terms of his function as Sophia's finest and final representative, as the mediator of eschatological and divine revelation. There is a large deposit of tradition belonging to such circles in Q, and Matthew takes this tradition quite seriously. His reaction is not wholly polemic, for he finds Wisdom ideology congenial to his own understanding of the gospel. However, the evangelist is at pains to correct this tradition in certain ways. First, he brings the tradition within the framework of the passion-dominated gospel form. Second—and this has not only claimed a major share of attention up to this point, but it will require further consideration under the discussion of the law—Matthew proceeds to an identification of Jesus with Sophia. It now becomes apparent that the long-recognized sayings belonging to the wisdom tradition are not merely outcroppings above the surface of Matthean Christology. As it had previously done for Paul and subsequently did for John, speculation about the pre-existent Sophia constituted an important element in Matthew's understanding of Christ.

IV. Wisdom and Law in the Gospel of Matthew

Come to me, all who labor and are heavy-laden, and I will give you rest. Take my yoke upon you, and learn from me; for I am gentle and lowly in heart, and you will find rest for your souls. For my yoke is easy, and my burden is light (Matt. 11:28–30).

This saying is universally regarded as belonging to the familiar genre of Wisdom's invitation. This means, as we have already seen, that Matthew, if he understood the Wisdom material at all—and it is clear that he did, has introduced it here as another saying in which Wisdom is identified with Christ. That is, it simply will not do to refer to it—as Bultmann does—as "the teacher making his appeal."[1] The first person of this invitation is the first person of Wisdom, not of her representative. No *sophos* invites men to take his yoke;

1. Rudolf Bultmann, *The History of the Synoptic Tradition*, tr. John Marsh (New York: Harper and Row, 1963), p. 159; contrast, G. von Rad, *Old Testament Theology*, tr. D. M. G. Stalker (Edinburgh and London: Oliver and Boyd, 1965), 2: 334–335.

rather he counsels men to accept the yoke of Sophia. The *sophos* promises that men will find rest; only Sophia can promise to give rest. Just as in Matt. 23:34–36 Jesus (as incarnate Wisdom) can speak Sophia's oracle of doom, or in 23:37–39 he can (in the same role) utter Wisdom's lament, so—in this place—Jesus issues Wisdom's invitation. His ἐγώ and the ἐγώ of Sophia are one. As Krister Stendahl has said, the Wisdom literature "seems to have been studied in the school of Matthew and related to Jesus, equating him with Wisdom."[2]

The Yoke of Wisdom and the Yoke of Jesus

The dominant theme of the passage is the "yoke." In the context of this investigation, the interpretation of the saying will, therefore, turn on the understanding given to the "yoke of Wisdom." And that, of course, will depend in large measure on how Wisdom is defined.

Tomas Arvedson, for example, examines the term "yoke" in the light of mystery terminology and declares for a fully cultic and mythological understanding in which the Isis myth is especially important. Arvedson writes:

If we now turn back to Sir. 6:18 ff., we find that the points of contact are really striking. As Isis at first confronts her worshipper with hard demands, so also does Wisdom. In both cases, the first level is conceived as a slavery, an imprisonment; the second, on the contrary, as a relation of love. In both cases what is designated by the picture of the yoke is symbolized by a priestly robe. That can hardly mean anything else than that the Isis mystery is directly or indirectly the basis of Sirach's details ... We are therefore to interpret the metaphor in Sir. 6:24 ff. accordingly. Whoever takes on himself the yoke or the fetters of Wisdom—that is, becomes her slave, her prisoner, her property—she makes her son and bridegroom; indeed, he becomes she herself. In this way she also unites him with Jahweh, for the service of Wisdom is also a service of Jahweh.[3]

2. Krister Stendahl, *The School of St. Matthew* (Uppsala: C. W. K. Gleerup, 1954), p. 142. Stendahl's observation was made in relation to Matt. 11:29, 27:43 and Stendahl's point turns on the influence of Sirach on Matthew's use of Jer. 6:16 in Matt. 11:29.

3. Tomas Arvedson, *Das Mysterium Christi: Eine Studie zu Mt. 11. 25–30* (Uppsala and Leipzig: Lundequistska bokhandeln and A. Lorentz, 1937), p. 200.

Now, it is quite probable that certain traits of personified Wisdom have been borrowed from Isis—as well as other goddesses in various periods, but many of the features have become quite at home in the Wisdom atmosphere. The only question that is involved at this point is whether the figure of Wisdom in Sirach and the related literature has become a Jewish mystery goddess with an accompanying cult.[4] That another line of development is taken here is largely due to the fact that, contrary to Arvedson, I think that the materials under consideration are not cult-related in this manner and that they are somewhat less further along on the road toward Gnosticism than he assumes. The striking parallels to Matt. 11:28–30 in Sirach 6 and 51 emanate, I think, from the school rather than the cult—from the inspired σοφός, who is not a mystagogue unless that term is used very loosely.

In Sirach 6, for example, Wisdom is personified; but, for Sirach, she is still somehow identified with the instruction of the school. Verses 24–31 cannot be separated from verses 18–22.

(18) My son, from your youth up choose instruction,
    and until you are old you will keep finding wisdom.
(19) Come to her like one who plows and sows,
    and wait for her good harvest.
For in her service you will toil a little while,
    and soon you will eat of her produce . . .
(22) For wisdom is like her name,[5]
    and is not manifest to many . . .

4. The attempts made to delineate a Jewish mystery in Philo are, to say the least, intriguing (Josef Pascher, *Η ΒΑΣΙΛΙΚΗ ΟΔΟΣ* [Paderborn: Ferdinand Schöningh, 1931], and E. R. Goodenough, *By Light, Light* [New Haven: Yale University Press, 1935]). Doubtless Philo stands in the Wisdom stream, and doubtless his interpretation of Judaism has been heavily influenced by an environment in which mysteries were important. Yet, it does not seem to me that the Jewish mystery has been established. If, for example, all of Goodenough's qualifications of the form of mystery piety in Philo are taken as seriously as the thesis which they qualify, then Goodenough has not really done more than illuminate the influence of the great Alexandrian's environment on the language used to interpret Judaism. At any rate Philo stands outside—or, better, beyond—the stream important for understanding Q and Matthew. Philo offers another goal toward which the development is moving, not an example of the central stream of wisdom and apocalyptic material which flowed into the primitive church.

5. Hebrew: "המוסר is like its name." A pun is involved. מוסר may be read "discipline" ("instruction"), or "fetter." The choice of σοφία to translate מוסר is unusual, but it is not inappropriate to the sense of the passage. "Wisdom" *is* "instruction," and one must put his "feet into her fetters."

101

(24) Put your feet into her fetters,
and your neck into her collar.
(25) Put your shoulder under her and carry her,
and do not fret under her bonds.
(26) Come to her with all your soul,
and keep her ways with all your might . . .
(28) For at last you will find the rest she gives,
and she will be changed into joy for you.
(29) Then her fetters will become for you a strong protection,
and her collar a glorious robe.
(30) Her yoke is a golden ornament,
and her bonds are a cord of blue.
(31) You will wear her like a glorious robe,
and put her on like a crown of gladness.

Whatever the source of this imagery, there can really be no doubt that the invitation extended on behalf of Wisdom is an invitation to instruction. Nor can there be any doubt that for Sirach this instruction is instruction in the Torah.

Sirach 51 offers the closest parallel to our passage. While we have seen that this hymn is an independent unit for which Sirach 6 cannot be determinative, the high incidence of the language of mysticism must not be allowed to obscure the plain significance of the wisdom teacher's concluding invitation:

Draw near to me, you who are untaught,
and lodge in my school . . .
Get (Wisdom) for yourselves without money.
Put your neck under the yoke,
and let your souls receive instruction;
it is to be found close by.
See with your eyes that I have labored little
and found for myself much rest. (51:23-27)

The reference in this passage to the " close by " Wisdom is, as Windisch recognized,[6] an allusion to Deut. 30:11-14 which speaks of the Torah as " the word near you "; thus, once again, a passage which includes an invitation to take up Wisdom's yoke is seen to be related both to school instruction and the

---

6. H. Windisch, *The Meaning of the Sermon on the Mount*, tr. S. M. Gilmour (Philadelphia: Westminster, 1951), pp. 99-100.

Torah. T. W. Manson comments on Sirach 51 quite correctly:

> It is clear that what is meant there is the yoke of the Law; for the "house of instruction" in v. 23 is nothing else but the *Beth ha-Midrash*, the school of the Law . . . Devotion to the Law of God sets a man free from the cares and troubles of the world. The Law in this sense is the written Law plus the interpretation given in the "house of instruction."[7]

In these passages we are introduced to an aspect of Jewish Wisdom speculation which is quite central, but which until now has been mentioned only in passing. This is the matter of Wisdom's relation to the law.[8] In its treatment of Wisdom and law, the wisdom literature prepares the way for the common Rabbinic identification of the two; it is, in fact, the source of that Rabbinic doctrine. Indeed, the close relation between the two is to be found even in the Wisdom of Solomon, where in some respects it is not to be expected. So, in "Solomon's" prayer, we find him saying:

> With thee is wisdom, who knows thy works
> and was present when thou didst make the world,
> and who understands what is pleasing in thy sight
> and what is right according to thy commandments. (9:9)

"Solomon" reproaches the mighty of the earth

> Because as servants of his kingdom you did not rule rightly,
> nor *keep the law*,
> nor walk according to the purpose of God . . .
> To you then, O monarchs, my words are directed
> that you may *learn wisdom and not transgress*. (6:4, 9)

---

7. T. W. Manson, "The Sayings of Jesus," in *The Mission and Message of Jesus* by H. D. A. Major, T. W. Manson, and C. J. Wright (New York: E. P. Dutton, 1938), p. 478.

8. I regret that when Ulrich Luck, *Die Vollkommenheitsforderung der Bergpredigt*, Theologische Existenz heute 150 (Munich: Chr. Kaiser, 1968) came to my attention this book was too far along in its progress at the press to make use of Luck's essay. The fact that the aperture through which Luck views Matthew is essentially anthropological while mine is basically Christological means that the place of the wisdom tradition in the Gospel is illuminated from two perspectives and quite independently. 103

In a judgment scene which has points of resemblance with passages concerning the vindication of the Son in Wisdom of Solomon, the Syriac Apocalypse of Baruch says:

Also (as for) the glory of those who have now been justified in My law, who have had understanding in their life, and who have planted in their heart the root of wisdom, then their splendour shall be glorified . . . For over this above all shall those who come then lament, that they rejected My law, and stopped their ears that they might not hear wisdom or receive understanding . . .

> But to those who have been saved by their works,
> And to whom the law has been now a hope,
> And understanding an expectation
> And wisdom a confidence,
> Shall wonders appear in their time. (51:3–4, 7)

Similarly the seer claims (38:4), "Thou knowest that my soul hath always walked in Thy law, and from my (earliest) days I departed not from Thy wisdom."

In these passages, neither wisdom nor law are cosmic figures; a similar relation of law and wisdom—where the two are identified in keeping with late wisdom doctrine, yet without personification—is to be found in the Testament of Levi 13.

Of interest in this connection are W. H. Brownlee's remarks on a Qumran Isaiah Scroll:

In the complete Isaiah Scroll occurs an interesting correction: the word *dabhar* of l. 4 seems to have been corrected to *dibbur*. The former may refer to the word of either man or God; but the latter term is a Rabbinic word meaning divine revelation, especially the Torah. The corrector may have been influenced by the Targum, where one reads: "The Lord God has given me the tongue of them that teach, to make me know how to teach *wisdom* to the righteous who faint for words of His *Torah*."[9]

The relation between wisdom and law may explain the appearance of "Unrighteousness" in the place of "Dame Folly" in 1 Enoch 42, a passage of which frequently only half

9. W. H. Brownlee, "Messianic Motifs in Qumran and the New Testament," *New Testament Studies*, 3 (1957), 20.

is cited. After speaking of Wisdom's vain quest for a resting place among men, with her resultant return to heaven, the passage tells how:

> Unrighteousness went forth from her chambers:
> Whom she sought not she found,
> And dwelt with them,
> As rain in a desert
> And dew on thirsty land.

Even more pointed is the relation between Wisdom and Torah in the praises of Wisdom found in Sirach and Baruch, both of which have fully laid the foundation for the later Rabbinic development. Here we meet the only case in which a pre-Christian "incarnation" of Wisdom may be spoken of with confidence. The prophets of Wisdom are inspired by her, have intimate fellowship with her, mediate wisdom; but the source of revelation in these cases remains Wisdom (or God). The Torah is another matter. It *is* Wisdom, the authority beyond which there is no need to appeal. Thus, Sirach 24 records a hymn in which Wisdom "praises herself."

> I came forth from the mouth of the Most High . . .
> I dwelt in high places . . .
> I sought in whose territory I might lodge . . .
> Then the Creator of all things gave me commandment . . .
> And he said, "Make your dwelling in Jacob . . ."
> In the holy tabernacle I ministered before him . . .
> In the beloved city likewise he gave me a resting place . . .
> Come to me, you who desire me,
>   and eat your fill of my produce . . .
> All this is the book of the covenant of the Most High God,
>   the law which Moses commanded us
>   as an inheritance for the congregations of Jacob . . .
>   (verses 3, 4, 7, 10, 11, 19, 23)

This full identification of Wisdom and law occurs in a passage in which even the language is reminiscent of the Johannine, "The Word became flesh and dwelled among us." Similarly, in Baruch 3:9—4:4 appears a passage in which Wisdom is extolled. It begins, "Hear the commandments of 105 life, O Israel; give ear and learn wisdom." Then, the inaccessibility of Wisdom is dealt with in a long passage somewhat in the vein of Job 28; its theme is that "no one knows the way to her" except God "who found the whole way to knowledge and gave her to Jacob his servant." The climax is reached with the definition: "She is the book of the commandments of God, and the law that endures forever" (3: 37—4: 1).

It is only against this background that Matt. 11:28–30 can be interpreted. The invitation which Jesus offers is the old invitation of Wisdom, and the yoke which is offered is the yoke of Wisdom, the yoke of the Torah. From this same source, the Rabbis also learned to speak of "the yoke of the law."[10] The first-century Rabbi Nehunia ben ha-Kanah reportedly said, "Every one who receives upon him the yoke of Torah, they remove from him the yoke of the kingdom and the yoke of worldly occupation. And every one who breaks off from him the yoke of Torah, they lay upon him the yoke of the kingdom and the yoke of worldly occupation."[11]

Jesus, Sophia, and the Torah

We should be very clear that in the Matthean setting what is offered by Jesus is *not* an alternative to the yoke of the Torah. Jesus speaks *as* Sophia, and in such a saying as 11: 28–30 that means *as* Torah as well. Rejection neither of the law nor of authoritative interpretation as a part of the law is implied in principle. To be sure, Matt. 23:4 says of the Pharisees and scribes that "they bind heavy burdens and lay them on men's shoulders," and this unmistakably refers to Pharisaic *Halakah*; it is still acknowledged that the scribes "sit on Moses' seat," which gives them the authority of legal

10. Arvedson, *Das Mysterium Christi*, p. 179, n. 4, considers the Rabbinic usage as "without doubt an imitative formation based on the usage in the wisdom literature."

11. R. Travers Herford, "Pirke Aboth," in *The Apocrypha and Pseudepigrapha of the Old Testament*, vol. 2, *Pseudepigrapha*, ed. R. H. Charles (Oxford: Clarendon, 1913), p. 699, comments: "The meaning is that devotion to Torah frees a man from oppression and care by setting his mind on things above; while if he despises Torah he feels all the weight of political oppression and struggle for existence." For additional examples see H. L. Strack and P. Billerbeck, *Das Evangelium nach Matthäus, Kommentar zum Neuen Testament aus Talmud und Midrasch* 1 (München: C. H. Beck, 1922), pp. 608–609.

pronouncement. Jesus' criticism is directed primarily against the hypocrisy involved when they lay such heavy burdens on men but do not themselves so much as "move them with their finger." Matt. 11:28–30 is not polemic against the law as such.

This becomes clear in the succeeding pericopes from Mark which Matthew has elected to insert in interpretative fashion following Wisdom's invitation. The first is the story of the disciples gathering grain on the Sabbath (Matt. 12:1–8), which Matthew has modified by introducing a more acceptable form of Rabbinic argumentation in support of the disciple's practice.[12] Matthew clearly acknowledges here that the issue involved is one of interpretation of Torah. Yet, he (like Luke) concludes the pericope simply with the saying "For the Son of man is Lord of the Sabbath," which means that for him the issue is really settled, not by exegetical subtlety, but by authoritative pronouncement. In this way, he ascribes to Jesus the authority to promulgate Torah.

Similarly, the next story, that of the healing of the man with the withered hand (Matt. 12:9–14), in no sense rejects the law. The pronouncement in this story makes the point that "it is permissible to do good on the sabbath," a direct statement in place of Mark's (and Luke's) repeated question, "Is it permissible on the sabbath to do good or to do harm?" E. Käsemann, in his "Beginnings of Christian Theology,"[13] has called attention to what amount to rival pronouncements by ecstatic prophets, some oriented toward Jewish Christianity and some toward the Hellenistic mission; in this connection he describes the rivalry vividily as "Spirit opposed to Spirit." What we confront in Matthew is law opposed to law. The yoke of Jesus is not some other yoke than the yoke of the Torah. Rather, the yoke of the true Torah, of Wisdom, is set over against that of Pharisaic Torah—as the two Sabbath pericopes clearly show.

If one law is here set above another, the "easy" yoke and

12. See David Daube, *The New Testament and Rabbinic Judaism* (London: Athlone, 1956), pp. 67–71. H. D. Betz, "The Logion of the Easy Yoke and of Rest," *Journal of Biblical Literature*, 86 (1967), 22, also sees the importance of Matt. 12:1–8 for the interpretation of our logion.

13. E. Käsemann, "Die Anfänge christlicher Theologie," *Zeitschrift für Theologie und Kirche*, 57 (1960), 166.

"light" burden do not imply the abolishing of the demands of the law. The idea that Wisdom's lordship is, in the end, gracious and life-giving, that it leads to "rest," is a regular feature of Wisdom's invitations, but it does not imply the absence of severe discipline and does frequently carry with it the notion of the pain of entering into Wisdom's service. "Solomon" rhapsodizes: "When I enter my house I shall find rest with her, for companionship with her has no bitterness, and life with her has no pain, but gladness and joy" (Wisd. of Sol. 8:16), but this is the testimony of a man who can speak with confidence of the salvation which company with Wisdom brings. Sirach 6 also confesses that "you will find the rest she gives" and that "her yoke is a golden ornament," but this confession is a testimony to what diligent service of Wisdom means. The context shows the author's awareness that it will not appear so to many. One must come to her "like one who plows and sows and wait for her good harvest." That means "putting your feet into her fetters, and your neck under her collar;" it means "keeping her ways with all your might." It is only in this kind of experience of Wisdom, this submissive meeting of Wisdom's demands, that "her fetters . . . become . . . a strong protection" and "her yoke . . . a golden ornament" (*cf.* Sir. 6: 19–31). That other poet who in Sirach 51 calls for bearing Wisdom's yoke, adding the testimony, "I have labored little and found for myself much rest," surely means: "I have labored little in comparison with the rest that I have found." Behind Wisdom's call in Matthew, "My yoke is easy," stands the obvious corollary that it will not seem so to everyone, that—in the words of Sir. 6:20—"she seems very harsh to the uninstructed; a weakling will not remain with her." The point of the succeeding illustrative narratives in Matthew is not so much that Jesus' yoke is "easy" in the sense that it amounts to a weakening of the law's demand, as that it is "easy" in the sense that it truly leads to life. There is no contradiction between the "easy yoke" and the stern demand: "Unless your righteousness exceeds that of the scribes and Pharisees, you will never enter the kingdom of heaven" (Matt. 5:20). In the end, the yoke which leads to rest and thus proves easy involves the higher righteousness.

The Sermon on the Mount

That brings us to the Sermon on the Mount. Opposite the first page of his massive volume on *The Setting of the Sermon on the Mount*, W. D. Davies set Matt. 11:28–30 with the notation: "The quintessence of the Matthean interpretation of Christianity as Gospel and Law." I would like to take that suggestion quite seriously and, proceeding from the understanding of Jesus as incarnate Wisdom-Torah sketched in connection with Matt. 11:28–30, consider its significance for a part of the Sermon on the Mount.

The procedure will be to examine the Sermon without either a condensed or running debate with other attempts to reach an over-all understanding of it (such as the widespread opinion that Jesus here appears as the New Moses on the New Sinai introducing a New Law). At specific points the conclusions of other investigators will be introduced, only when it is felt that they will advance the course of the discussion. One other word should be said. Although the presentation will make it obvious that some aspects of W. D. Davies's treatment of the Sermon have not convinced me, I should state in advance that my debt to him—especially to his *Paul and Rabbinic Judaism*—is exceedingly great.[14]

The Antitheses

The beginning point for treating the Sermon will be the antitheses of Matt. 5:21–48. The contrast between Jesus' "But I say unto you" and the prophetic "Thus saith the Lord," is frequently and correctly said to ascribe to him an unparalleled authority, beyond that of the prophets, at least equal with that of Moses. What has Matthew meant to say by placing this section as the first main part of the Sermon? The question must be put in this way because beyond

---

14. I have tried to avoid reading Rabbinic texts as sources of early Christian theology rather than as later products of a tradition-historical process of which the Rabbinic tradition is but one end-product. That is a corollary to my similar reluctance to use the materials of second- and third-century Gnosticism to illuminate the background of the discussion. For the most part the New Testament's background is to be sought, in my opinion, in the unstable components still in search of that resolution which Jamnia provided for most of Judaism and which catholic orthodoxy eventually furnished Christianity.

question, the antitheses in their present formulation belong to Matthew and must be presumed to have a special significance.[15]

Of course, the assertion of Matthean responsibility for the antithetical formulations has been challenged. Barth thinks that the "non-Q" sayings beginning at verses 21, 27, and 33 must have been pre-Matthean, "for in their case the antithesis without the thesis would be scarcely intelligible."[16] This is not quite self-evident. For example, the paragraph on adultery contains two verses (Matt. 5:29–30) for which parallels are found in both Mark (9:43–48) and Matthew (18:8–9). They, to be sure, are not a part of the antithesis proper (Matt. 5:27–28). Nevertheless, the question must be raised whether they are to be considered commentary brought to this location to illuminate the antithesis—or whether, alternatively, the antithesis has been created to provide a suitable setting for the sayings about the removal of offending organs of the body. If this latter suggestion is followed, the paragraph would be exactly parallel to the antithesis on retribution and nonretaliation (Matt. 5:38–42), which Barth thinks was "formulated by Matthew himself" because it is not antithetically formulated in Q. However, if Barth is correct about this logion derived from Q, then Matthew has created the whole saying, "You have heard that it was said, 'An eye for an eye . . .' But I say to you, Do not resist one who is evil," in order to provide an antithetical setting for the logion concerning turning the other cheek, surrendering the cloak, walking the second mile, and giving to the beggar. Something like this would also explain the antithesis in verses 27–30.

In neither of the other two non-Q instances is it at all clear that the saying would have to be preserved in an antithetical form. The core of Matt. 5:22 (the ruling on murder) is a

---

15. The following discussion presupposes the existence of Q. However, even if Matthew rather than Q is the source of Luke's parallels, the artful arrangement of the antitheses following Matt. 5:17–20 is redactional, for the antitheses must be regarded as a kind of commentary on verses 17–20, which—on form-critical grounds alone—can only be treated as an editorial combination of diverse traditions.

16. G. Barth, "Matthew's Understanding of the Law," in Günther Bornkamm, Gerhard Barth, and H. J. Held, *Tradition and Interpretation in Matthew*, tr. P. Scott (Philadelphia: Westminster, 1963), p. 93.

graduated sequence of rulings which is appropriate enough in its present setting, but quite capable of standing independently without a prefixed "But I say unto you." Verses 34–37 have partial parallels in familiar New Testament texts (Matt. 23:16–22, James 5:12), not to mention Philo (On the Decalogue II. I–III), none of which are formulated antithetically. On the other hand, the saying about love of enemies (Matt. 5:43–48) which appears to be from Q, is introduced by an ἀλλά in the parallel in Luke 6:27. The adversative strikes a jarring note at its location in Luke, but the absence of a negative in the preceding Matthean thesis (which is to be expected with ἀλλά) does not really encourage the suspicion of a lost antithetical construction in Luke. I think it is best to regard the whole series as constructed by Matthew.[17]

If this series has been constructed by Matthew, do the antitheses conform to a pattern which would make them of little Christological significance? That is, does Matthew simply accommodate Jesus' speech to a form of Rabbinic discourse because of his interest in Jesus as a teacher? Morton Smith and David Daube have each proposed that the antitheses can be understood in terms of types of Rabbinic discussion. Smith cites a number of passages in which divergent Rabbinic opinions are stated under the rubrics: "R. So-and-so used to say... But I say..."[18] Attractive as Smith's argument is, the parallels are not quite convincing. In the first place, the passages he cites are parallel only to the second half of the antithesis. Of course, it is perfectly true, as Smith reminds us, that both the expressions "You have heard" and "It was said" are to be found in Rabbinic material. But he does not cite an example of a passage in which the "You have heard" formula appears in connection with "But I say"; the parallel exists for only half of the Matthean construction.[19]

17. It is clear at least that the Q sayings in this group were remembered in a nonantithetical form; cf. Barth, *Tradition and Interpretation*, p. 93.

18. Morton Smith, *Tannaitic Parallels to the Gospels*, Journal of Biblical Literature Monograph 6 (Philadelphia: Society of Biblical Literature, 1951), pp. 27–30.

19. That this point is important to Smith as well is shown by the fact that he devotes a long paragraph to the formula which is missing from his examples. He is particularly interested in explaining Matt. 5:21 ("You have heard that it was said *to the men of old*"). He objects to Delling's understanding of this in terms of Rabbinic

In the second place, the "I say to you" of the examples given by Smith appears in a particular setting, namely that of scholarly discussion. In spite of one Pharisaic teacher's claim to be "the first of all those who come after me," and Smith's conviction that Jesus was not "the only self-confident Rabbi,"[20] one simply would not think of making a collection of Rabbi Simon ben Yohai's dissents from Rabbi Akiba and closing the collection with the sentence, "He taught them as one who had authority, and not as their scribes" (Matt. 7:29). It does not seem credible that Matthew's intention at this point was to represent Jesus' authoritative proclamation as mere academic debate.

Daube has isolated a Rabbinic form which runs: "I might understand (hear) . . . but you must say."[21] Daube himself calls attention to the gulf between what he calls "a scholarly working out by some Rabbis of a progressive interpretation" and what he calls "a laying down by Jesus, supreme authority, of the proper demand,"[22] which the "but I say to you" represents. And Stendahl remarks that Matthew 5 "differs from such usage strikingly when Jesus turns it around and claims his own authority . . . Such a form presupposes an authority far beyond that of the scribes."[23]

The problem of understanding the antitheses is complicated by the ambiguous attitude toward the law which early Christian tradition attests. Granted that the problem has taken on a special coloring in Paul, the ambiguity is nonetheless illustrated by the fact that it takes a skillful exegete to move a class of seminarians past Paul's statement, "So the law is holy, and the commandment is holy and just and good" (Rom. 7:12), without debate. Matthew's presentation of Jesus' relation to the law makes jugglers of all of us. On the

---

references to ancient worthies, since the Tannaitic literature "always declares that *they* said or did something, and not that something was said to them." His own solution is to read Matt. 5:21 in terms of a related Rabbinic expression which is to be translated, "*At first* they used to say . . ." which was followed by the explanation that "they came round to saying" something else; but that is not parallel, either. (See Smith, *Tannaitic Parallels*, pp. 27–30.)

20. *Tannaitic Parallels*, p. 30.

21. *New Testament and Rabbinic Judaism*, pp. 55–60.

22. *New Testament and Rabbinic Judaism*, p. 58.

23. K. Stendahl, "Matthew," in *Peake's Commentary on the Bible*, ed. M. Black and H. H. Rowley (New York: Thomas Nelson and Sons, 1962), p. 776.

one hand, the discussion of divorce in 19:3–9 proceeds along the lines of Rabbinic argumentation; it concludes in verses 8–9 with a contrast between Moses' teaching and Jesus' "I say unto you" which recalls the pattern discussed by Smith. On the other hand, the antithesis on divorce in 5:31–32 has no patience with debate and is formulated as sheer pronouncement in such a way that many scholars regard it as direct abrogation of the law. Or, again, while the first and second antitheses give the appearance of simply making the law more stringent, the remainder can be interpreted as abolishing the law. There is also the added fact that, while most of the antitheses seem to be aimed at a prevailing interpretation of the law, some take their point of departure directly from the written Torah.

The tensions are so great even within very limited sections of Matthew, for example, that G. Bornkamm decides that Matthew was not

aware of the inconsistency between these antitheses and the binding force of the 'letter' as stated in the Judaistic Jewish-Christian formulation of vv. 18f., which was firmly held down to the jot and tittle. His allegiance to Jesus' own words and to the understanding of the law in the Judaistic Jewish-Christian tradition stand here in unmistakable tension with each other.[24]

It is very questionable whether an unrecognized inconsistency should be appealed to at this particular point. In the first place, the most troublesome antitheses are those which are manifestly Matthean creations as Barth has shown,[25] so that any assumption of "loyalty to Jesus' own words" is misplaced. Even if by "Jesus' own words" were meant, for example, only the saying on divorce, the addition of "but I say unto you" has so heightened the contrast that Matthew must have known what he was about. In the second place, while Barth regards verses 18–19 as pre–Matthean, he properly insists "that Matthew does not simply take over the sayings about the law (5.18f.) and pass them on" but uses

24. G. Bornkamm, "End-Expectation and Church in Matthew," in *Tradition and Interpretation*, p. 25.

25. *Tradition and Interpretation*, p. 93.

them polemically against Christians who have a lax attitude toward the law.[26] There is too much of Matthew himself in this section to rely on an uncritical collection of divergent traditions to explain the tension.

What is involved is not Matthew's failure to recognize an inconsistency, but rather an arbitrary manner of dealing with the Torah. For Matthew, there is no inconsistency because whether the law in either written or oral expression is now being corrected, extended, or fulfilled, the whole matter falls under an authority by which alone the proper interpretation of the law and its literal establishment alike are determined. At the points where we feel an inconsistency, Matthew knows no problem at all because he appeals *always* to the Torah even when he appears to contradict it. For him, Jesus is Wisdom-Torah.

There is, therefore, no contradiction between a ruling of Jesus and the "letter of the Torah." There is no question of the authority of Jesus versus the authority of the Torah. There is only the question of true Torah (which in its "jot and tittle" can only agree with and testify to Wisdom) and false Torah (which for Matthew means the law falsely understood). Therefore, Jesus' teaching may on the one hand be proved from the law or on the other be asserted as sheer authoritative legal pronouncement. The Torah, when it is rightly understood, can only testify to itself. The "I say unto you" of Matthew 5 is not intended to abolish the law. It may, in a sense, extend and deepen the requirements of the law, but that is not its intent either. It is, instead, the authoritative declaration of what in fact the law is. Loisy was on the right track when to his treatment of Matt. 11:25–30 he appended the suggestion that "the identification of Jesus with Wisdom may explain the tone of the antitheses."[27]

In a discussion of Kilpatrick's claim that "the central position that Judaism gave to the law, the Gospel gives to Jesus," Bornkamm rightly objects to Kilpatrick's false inference that this means that for Matthew the law has "an

---

26. *Tradition and Interpretation*, p. 71.

27. A. Loisy, *Les Évangiles Synoptiques* (Ceffonds, Montier-en-Der [Haute-Marne], 1907–1908), 1: 913; T. Preiss, "Jésus et la Sagesse," *Études Théologiques et Religieuses*, 28, (1953), 71: "Jésus s'est mis délibérément à la place de la Thora elle-même. En fait cet *ἐγώ* solennel est celui de Dieu, ou, pour le moins, de sa Thora."

important, though subordinate place in the Christian scheme." Then Bornkamm continues:

The saying in Matt. 18.20 can, in fact, say of Jesus what the Rabbis correspondingly said of the Torah (*Pirke Aboth* 3.2, 'when two sit (together) and there are words of the Torah between them, there the Shekina sojourns between them'), and Matthew also puts sayings from the Wisdom literature into the mouth of Jesus. This does not mean that Jesus is put *in the place* of the law (or Wisdom), but rather, in the sense of 5.17ff., is the confirmation of the law.[28]

Of course, Jesus is not "put in the place of Wisdom-Torah" in the sense that he displaces it, but to say of him what the Rabbis say of the Torah or to attribute to him oracles of Wisdom does, if it is meant seriously, "put him in the place of Wisdom-Torah" in the more important sense we are proposing here. Even if we were to regard the anti-theses as formulated on a Rabbinic model, it would be impossible to treat them as the alternative interpretation of a superior Rabbi. In the Matthean context, the "I say unto you" claims what no scribal authority could claim, and this is especially important in view of the seriousness with which Matthew takes the authority of the scribe. Daube describes a gulf of unbridgable breadth when he writes: "Jesus, supreme authority, lays down the proper demand: this accounts for 'But I say unto you, That whosoever is angry, etc. . . .' The setting in life of the Rabbinic form is a dialectic exposition of the Law; that of the Matthean is proclamation of the true Law."[29] And I would add: the authority which is here called supreme is none other than that of the Torah itself, who in the Sermon on the Mount challenges men to take up the yoke, to obey.

Matt. 5:17–20: The Permanence of the Law

Does this discussion shed any light on what it means in Matt. 5:17 for Jesus to say, "I have come . . . to fulfill the

---

28. *Tradition and Interpretation*, p. 35, n. 2; *cf.* G. D. Kilpatrick, *The Origins of the Gospel According to St. Matthew* (Oxford: Clarendon, 1950), pp. 108–109.
29. *New Testament and Rabbinic Judaism*, p. 59.

law and the prophets"?[30] Probably less than we should hope. In a certain sense, it might be thought to lend support to the occasional interpretation of "fulfill" as meaning "establish," although the philological grounds for this translation do not appear to be solid.[31] It is also obvious that from our perspective Matthew presents a "deepened" understanding of the law, based on the commandment to love, so that the rendering of "fulfill" by "complete" is not unattractive. Ljungmann's proposal to interpret Matt. 5:17–20 in the light of his special interpretation of Matt. 3:15, so that $\pi\lambda\eta\rho\tilde{\omega}\sigma\alpha\iota$ would imply the "filling" of scripture in the self-surrender of the Messiah (which means the forgiveness of sins and the coming of that "righteousness" which his disciples are both to receive and to do), falls short of being convincing.[32] It is not that Ljungmann has described an un-Matthean view of the work of Christ, but that he imports too much into the language of this particular passage. None of these interpretations would be "at war" with our understanding of Matthew's position on the law. To some degree, any one of them is capable of complementing the view that Christ is to be identified with Wisdom-Torah. On the whole, however, I have been unable to convince myself that the definitive answer is to be found among them.

Nor do I have a final answer to propose as to the significance of the term "fulfill" in verse 17. The question is complicated by the fact that Matt. 5:17–20 comprises four sayings which do not appear to have any pre-Matthean connection with each other. Verse 18 is drawn from Q (Luke 16:17). The absence of an antecedent for "these commandments" in verse 19 is enough to show its independence of verse 18. Verses 19 and 20 are to be distinguished on the grounds that in the former, opponents are depicted who will be "least" in the Kingdom, while the latter has in view opponents who certainly will not enter the Kingdom at all. Moreover, the application of purely formal criteria sets verse

---

30. For convenient summaries of various opinions, see H. Ljungmann, *Das Gesetz erfüllen*, Lunds Universitets Årsskrift, n. f. 50 (Lund: C. W. K. Gleerup, 1954), pp. 19–36, and E. P. Blair, *Jesus in the Gospel of Matthew* (New York: Abingdon, 1960), pp. 117–122.

31. Ljungmann, *Das Gesetz erfüllen*, pp. 29–33.

32. *Das Gesetz erfüllen*, passim.

19 apart.[33] Verse 17 is placed at the head of this group of sayings and may be Matthean in origin: the form μὴ νομίσητε ὅτι ἦλθον . . . οὐκ ἦλθον . . . ἀλλά . . . also appears at Matt. 10:34. These sayings have been assembled by Matthew to form a new unity, the exact meaning of which is obscured by the uncertainty of "fulfill" in verse 17 and of the editorial phrase "until all things come to be" in verse 18.

Thus, our primary positive understandings of Matthew's view of the relation of Christ to the law will have to be derived from other passages. This is not because Matthew did not intend to be clear, but it is simply the blunt recognition that at the present moment no clear preference among several alternative interpretations has commanded a consensus. We decide what "fulfill" and "until all things come" mean on the basis of what we find in Matthew outside of these two sentences, which makes it difficult to use these sentences in a normative fashion for treating the subject.

I am inclined to think that one of two interpretations not previously mentioned here is probably correct. The first would find its clue in Matt. 7:12 and 22:40, in both of which the commandment of love is spoken of as the sum of the law and the prophets. Here, as frequently happens in the Rabbis, the prophets are thought of as explicating the law. In a sense "the prophets legislate"—or, at least, they teach Torah. On this approach, it is most natural to understand "fulfill" as meaning to "do" what the law commands, to satisfy its requirements. This appears to be what Paul means in Rom. 13:8–10, when he says that: "He who loves his neighbor has fulfilled the law," and "Love is the fulfilling of the law," as well as in Gal. 5:14. In view of Rom. 8:3–4 and Paul's treatment of the law in general, it may be suggested that in these two passages Paul preserves a traditional formulation which provides the answer to the quite practical question, "How is the law to be satisfied?" If we take "fulfill" in Matt. 5:17 to mean "do" what the law requires, then the phrase "until all comes to pass" in 5:18 would probably mean something like "until the law is fully done." Jesus would then take his place as the defender and upholder of the law, who does not propose its abolition but affirms its

33. See Käsemann, *Zeitschrift für Theologie und Kirche,* 57 (1960), 165.

eternity; "not a jot or a tittle shall disappear from it" but it shall exist until "heaven and earth pass away."

If that is not what the sayings are about, then I am inclined to think they speak very directly—almost crudely—of the fulfillment of what has been prophesied of the Messiah. I do not intend to develop an exposition of Matthew's full Christology.[34] However, it is obvious that there are elements of a more conventional messianic doctrine to which the Wisdom aspect must be accommodated. The interchangeability of "deeds of the Christ" and "deeds of Wisdom" in 11:2, 19 shows that—whatever special meaning the term "Christ" has for Matthew—it is precisely the Messiah who is Wisdom incarnate. That the multiple components of Matthew's Christology are in tension, that they are even unharmonious, would not make the evangelist an exceptional first-century "theologian"! For the interpretation presently under discussion, we would simply have to accept the idea that Matthew in this saying thinks of Jesus as the one in whom the promises of the past come to pass. In this light "the law and the prophets" is to be understood as in Matt. 11:13, where (notice the inverted order) it is said that "the prophets and the law prophesied until John"—implying that since John the prophecy is being fulfilled.[35] It of course requires no extensive proof to say that the law "prophesies." To cite only one of the subtler examples, Rom. 3:21 speaks of the testimony of "the law and the prophets" to the righteousness which is not based on law—and Paul then demonstrates what he means by using a typological exegesis of Pentateuchal material in chapter 4. This understanding of Matt. 5:17 would accord with the meaning "fulfill" which, because of its employment in the citation formulas, is the predominant meaning of the term in our Gospel. On this understanding, the law and the prophets are a unity of legislation and prediction; and verse 17 may be paraphrased, "Do not think I came to destroy the law *or* the prophets. I

---

34. *Cf.* Blair, *Jesus in the Gospel of Matthew.*

35. This is not, of course, the meaning of the parallel in Luke 16:16, which may set a term to the validity of the law. It is, however, plainly the meaning of Matthew, as discussed above, Barth's ingenious attempt (*Tradition and Interpretation,* p. 64) to explain Matthew's alteration of the Q saying as due to the evangelist's affirmation of the eternal validity of the law, notwithstanding.

came to fulfill the promises of Scripture. Can the one who fulfills Scripture's prophecies really be thought its enemy?" Verse 18 would then mean, "Until heaven and earth pass away, not a jot or a tittle will pass away from the law, for all that is promised in it must come to pass." The Scripture is a unity. If Christ is to fulfill its predictions, then he must also stand as the guarantor of the validity of its commandments.

Whatever positive declaration about Jesus' relation to the law was intended by Matthew, it is clear that these declarations were meant to enhance in the strongest possible way Matthew's insistence that Jesus was not the enemy of the law. The words, "Do not think that I have come to destroy the Law," clearly imply a contrary opinion which Matthew is at pains to contradict.[36] The statement is made, therefore, out of polemic or apologetic intent. That is, the claim may have been made by some party in the Church that the law was no longer wholly in effect for Christians, or the charge may have been levelled by Jews that Jesus had sought to abolish the law. It is not entirely impossible that Matthew has opponents of both varieties in view, since it can be shown that Matthew's teaching on the law was directed against the lax observance of the law both in the church and in Pharisaism. Thus, Käsemann is correct when he says of our passage that, although it is " the subject of lively controversy," it is essentially "unambiguous and commands obedience to the whole Torah right up to the last jot."[37]

The antitheses which follow cannot be understood as a contradiction of this demand, for, as we have seen, Matthew's intention in the antitheses is not to defeat the law but to define it. In principle, Matthew has broken through the tension between the law and the life of the Spirit. Christ is not set over against the law, but identified with it.

Yet, law is opposed to law, interpretation to interpretation. Matthew's elevation of the love-commandment to a place of normative significance in his interpretation of the law raises the question in what sense the "last jot" of Torah is really significant for him. Is it possible that Käsemann is right in saying that Matthew "can no longer understand literally,

36. Cf. Barth, Tradition and Interpretation, p. 67.
37. Zeitschrift für Theologie und Kirche, 57 (1960), 165.

as it was originally meant" the tradition about the eternal validity of the law? Says Käsemann, "He comments on it in the sense of the radical commandment of love."[38] That the love-commandment has determined the content of the law for Matthew does not require extensive treatment here. So much may be assumed. But Barth is surely correct in insisting that the elevation of the commandment of love which makes it possible to claim that *this* rather than *that* is the true Torah has Christological roots.[39] That is to say, what is involved here is not merely a principle of interpretation but the issue of authority, and Matthew's identification of Christ and Wisdom is central to that issue.

The Disciples as Scribes

This helps to account for the fact that those who are commissioned by Jesus in Matthew's Gospel are commissioned to a task which retains the law at its core. There are in Matthew three clear examples of commissionings of the disciples, only one of which is pre-Matthean.

First, Matt. 28:18–20, a passage closely akin to the hymn and invitation of 11:25–30, is the most obvious commission, and on the surface it calls upon the disciples to transmit the "law of Christ." The evangelists who are called to "preach the gospel" are also scribes who are called to "teach them to observe all that I have commanded you," while the promise to be "with you always" is reminiscent of the Wisdom saying in 18:20.

Second, there is the commissioning of Peter (16:17–19), old traditional material which has been taken over by Matthew.[40] It is important to notice that the commissioning

---

38. *Zeitschrift für Theologie und Kirche*, 57 (1960), 165. On the relation of the "rule of love" to the law in Matthew, see now also Charles E. Carlston, "The Things That Defile (Mark VII. 14) and the Law in Matthew and Mark," *New Testament Studies*, 15 (1968), 75–96, which appeared after this book was completed.

39. *Tradition and Interpretation*, p. 104.

40. This saying must have circulated first among Christians who spoke Aramaic. This is shown by the Semitic structure of the sentence (declaration followed by two clauses in antithetical parallelism), the fact that the word play on the name "Rock" comes off better in Aramaic than in Greek, the probable Jewish origin of the expression πύλαι ᾅδου, and the reference to flesh and blood in the beatitude. *Cf.* Bultmann, *History of the Synoptic Tradition*, pp. 138–140, and J. Jeremias, *Golgotha*, Angelos 1 (Leipzig: Eduard Pfeiffer, 1926), p. 69.

of Peter consists of three parts:
(1) The pronouncement of a benediction over the disciple (verse 17).

Blessed are you, Simon Bar-Jonah! For flesh and blood has not revealed this to you, but my Father who is in heaven.

(2) The bestowal of a new name, Rock, along with its interpretation (verse 18).

And I tell you, you are Rock, and on this rock I will build my church, and the powers of death shall not prevail against it.

(3) The commission proper (verse 19).

I will give you the keys of the kingdom of heaven, and whatever you bind on earth shall be bound in heaven, and whatever you loose on earth shall be loosed in heaven.

Matt. 23:13 (cf. Luke 11:52!) reinforces what the language of 16:19 itself confirms, namely that to Peter are committed what are essentially scribal functions.[41] The commission reflects a time when the ecstatic leader of the community was regarded as having the authority to declare the law[42] and is to be compared not with its parallel in 18:20 so much as with 5:19, where warning is given against "loosing one of the least of these commandments."

The existence of "prophets" and "scribes" in the Matthean community has been suggested on the basis of 23:34 ("I will send you prophets and wise men and scribes"); the

41. This is true whether "binding" and "loosing" are understood in relation to the right to declare legal decisions ("forbid," "permit") or to impose or remove the ban. See R. Hummel, *Die Auseinandersetzung zwischen Kirche und Judentum im Matthäusevangelium*, Beiträge zur evangelischen Theologie 33 (München: Chr. Kaiser, 1963), p. 62: "Diese Überlegungen führen zu dem Ergebnis, dass Matthäus unter 'Binden' und 'Lösen' wahrscheinlich die Vollmacht des Schriftgelehrten verstanden hat, die beides, Lehr- und Disziplinargewalt, umfasst, und dass er in 18, 18 auf die letztere, in 16, 19 aber auf erstere abhebt. Dann erscheint die Zitierung des Felsenwortes sinnvoll. Die Grundlage der Kirche ist für Matthäus das rechte Verständnis und die rechte Auslegung und Anwendung des Gesetzes."
42. *Cf.* Käsemann, *Zeitschrift für Theologie und Kirche*, 57 (1960), *passim*.

"prophet" is again mentioned in 5:12;[43] and the "scribe of the kingdom" (13:52) is described at the very close of the so-called Matthean "book of Wisdom" (11:2—13:53). In the light of this evidence, I want to suggest that 5:11–16 has been constructed by Matthew so as to form the first commissioning saying in the Gospel. The well-known problem of the shift from the third person in the beatitudes of 5:3–10 to the second person in that of 5:11–12 is to be explained as due to the fact that Matthew here moves from the beatitudes proper (which announce in a general way the conditions of entrance into the Kingdom)[44] to a commissioning of the disciples (who are the primary audience, although the subject matter of the Sermon is of universal validity).[45] This commission is made up of three independent sayings which Matthew has arranged to conform to the pattern of Peter's commission in chapter 16. It consists of the three elements previously identified in that passage:

(1) The benediction (5:11–12).

Blessed are you when men revile you and persecute you and utter all kinds of evil against you falsely on my account. Rejoice and be glad, for your reward is great in heaven, for so men persecuted the prophets who were before you.

(2) The bestowal of names (5:13–15).

You are the Salt of the earth, but if salt has lost its taste, how shall its saltness be restored? It is no longer good for anything except to be thrown out and trodden under foot by men. You are the Light of the world. A city set on a hill cannot be hid. Nor do men light a lamp and put it under a bushel, but on a stand, and it gives light to all in the house.

43. Kurt Schubert, "The Sermon on the Mount and the Qumran Texts," in K. Stendahl, ed., *The Scrolls and the New Testament* (New York: Harper, 1957), pp. 122–124, understands Matt. 5:12 to speak of Christian prophets and suggests Essene parallels.

44. *Cf.* Windisch, *The Meaning of the Sermon on the Mount*, pp. 27–29.

45. C. H. Dodd, "The Beatitudes," in *Mélanges Bibliques rédigés en l'honneur de André Robert* (Paris: Bloud et Gay, 1957), p. 405, writes: "It would appear therefore that the ninth beatitude was not conceived by the evangelist as an integral part of the series, which is indeed marked as a complete unit by the repetition after the eighth makarism, of the same clause as that which followed the first . . ."; also in C. H. Dodd, *More New Testament Studies* (Grand Rapids: Eerdmans, 1968), p. 2.

(3) The commission proper (5:16).

Let your light so shine before men, that they may see your good works and give glory to your Father who is in heaven.

(1) The benediction pronounces blessing on those who are persecuted, because "so men persecuted the prophets who were before you." This must be considered significant in view of Wisdom-Christ's promise in Matt. 23:34–36 to send "prophets, wise men, and scribes" who will be persecuted as were Wisdom's former prophets. Luke's parallel saying (6:23) concludes: "for so their fathers did to the prophets"; this signifies that, for Luke, the disciples share the prophets' lot but are not themselves described as prophets. However, Matthew's "prophets who were before you" shows the recipients of the benediction to be prophets themselves. McNeile's comment that the phrase τοὺς προφήτας τοὺς πρὸ ὑμῶν (Matt. 5:12) does not need to "imply that the disciples are reckoned as prophets" is like saying that in Gal. 1:17 the almost identically formed phrase, τοὺς πρὸ ἐμοῦ ἀποστόλους, need not imply that Paul was an apostle![46]

(2) The sayings "You are the Salt of the earth" and "You are the Light of the world" (Matt. 5:13, 14) are to be regarded as a bestowal of names which indicate the place of these prophets in the church, much as "You are Rock" does for Peter in chapter 16.[47] E. Norden regarded all three of these (5:13, 14; 16:18) as examples of an Oriental formula of address which is a correlate of the self-revelation formula ἐγώ εἰμι.[48] For both Matthew 16 and Matthew 5, the con-

46. A. H. McNeile, *The Gospel According to St. Matthew* (London, Macmillan, 1938), p. 54. Douglas R. A. Hare, *The Theme of Jewish Persecution of Christians in the Gospel according to St. Matthew*, Society for New Testament Studies Monograph Series 6 (Cambridge, England: Cambridge University Press, 1967), p. 116 (*cf.* p. 140, n. 4), declares: "As it stands the phrase clearly implies that those addressed stand directly in the prophetic tradition."

47. Oscar Cullmann, *Peter: Disciple, Apostle, Martyr*, 2nd ed. rev. (Philadelphia: Westminster, 1962), pp. 19–20, writes: "It corresponds to Jewish custom to choose as titles words which somehow point to the promise in a particular situation and lay an obligation on their bearer. We know such examples from the Old Testament, and in a similar way Jewish disciples also received from their Rabbi a title. Jesus himself gave such a title not only to Peter but also to the sons of Zebedee: *Boanerges.*"

48. E. Norden, *Agnostos Theos* (Stuttgart: Teubner, 1956), p. 185.

text is one of revelation; in Matthew 16 there is a revelation "by the Father," and in Matthew 5 there is the familiar mountain and the "I have come" saying. It is, therefore, not unreasonable to think of these sayings as "installation formulas" in some sense.

Matt. 5: 13–15 is unquestionably a Matthean formulation, as both the Marcan (4:21, 9:50) and Lucan (8:16, 11:33, 14:34–35) parallels show.[49] The fact that Matthew has chosen to transform sayings about "salt" and "light" into sayings patterned after the form "You are Rock" is particularly illuminating. Wolfgang Nauck in a study of salt as a metaphor for discipleship has clearly established that the salt metaphor as used here has its roots in Rabbinic instructions to disciples, in which "to be salted" means "to be wise."[50] This understanding is considerably strengthened by the fact that the passive of μωραίνω can be used both to mean "to become insipid" and "to become foolish," while the translation equivalents in Hebrew (תפל) and in Aramaic (טרי) also may mean "to become foolish" as well as "to become insipid."[51] Nauck understands our passage to mean that "Jesus calls his disciples the real teachers, the true wise men in opposition to the Jewish wise men."[52] The connection of the light metaphor with teachers of the law is also a familiar Jewish metaphor,[53] which recurs in Rom. 2:19 in a context the whole of which is relevant to our discussion.

But if you call yourself a Jew and rely upon the law and boast of your relation to God and know his will and approve what is excellent, because you are instructed in the law, and if you are sure that you are a guide to the blind, a light to those who are in darkness, a corrector of the foolish, a teacher of children, having in the

49. Cf. Bultmann, History of the Synoptic Tradition, p. 98.

50. Wolfgang Nauck, "Salt as a Metaphor in Instruction for Discipleship," Studia Theologica, 6 (1952), 165–178.

51. W. D. Davies, The Setting of the Sermon on the Mount (Cambridge, England: Cambridge University Press, 1964), p. 204, n. 1, cites a statement of R. Eliezer (A.D. 80–120) which includes the saying "The wisdom of the Scribes shall become insipid."

52. Studia Theologica, 6 (1952), 177; cf. Ljungmann, Das Gesetz erfüllen, p. 7.

53. Cf., for example, Test. Levi 14:4, Syr. Apoc. Bar. 77:13–16. In 11 QPs[a] xxvii, 2, David is described as a "wise man and a light" who spoke "through prophecy."

law the embodiment of knowledge and truth—you then who teach others, will you not teach yourselves? (Rom. 2:17–21).

Paul's words show the same concern as Matthew has for those who teach but do not practice. Thus, we are led to the recognition that, as in Matt. 28:20 the disciples are sent to teach men to observe commandments, and as in 16:19 Peter is assigned a specifically scribal task, so here in 5:13–15 the "prophets" are given names which designate them as "scribes and wise men."

This is not to say that for Matthew the "prophet" and "scribe" is an interpreter of the law and nothing else. Matt. 13:1–53, which closes with the parable of the scribe of the Kingdom,[54] is wholly concerned with the revelation of the "mystery" of the Kingdom to those who "understand."[55] Matthew allows to his scribe that full range of wisdom which Sirach describes:

> On the other hand he who devotes himself
> to the study of the law of the Most High
> will seek out the wisdom of the ancients,
>   and will be concerned with prophecies;
> he will preserve the discourse of notable men
>   and penetrate the subtleties of parables;
> he will seek out the hidden meaning of proverbs
>   and be at home with the obscurities of parables.
>
> (39:1–3).

The disciple of Jesus may say of his Lord what "Solomon" said of Wisdom:

> She knows the things of old, and infers the things to come;
> she understands turns of speech and the solution of riddles;
> she has foreknowledge of signs and wonders
> and of the outcome of seasons and times (Wisd. of Sol. 8:8).

There is an interesting correspondence between Matthew 5 and Matthew 23. In the latter passage, a series of seven

54. For the interpretation of Matthew 13, the whole of 4 Ezra is of particular importance.

55. On the use of "understand" in Matthew, see Barth, *Tradition and Interpretation*, pp. 105–112.

woes is followed by an oracle in which Wisdom promises to send "prophets and wise men and scribes"; there, emissaries who proclaim the end are clearly in view and the appearance of "wise men and scribes" is a little strange in a context which makes us think of scribes as "Pharisaic scribes."[56] In Matthew 5, a series of seven[57] beatitudes is followed by a commissioning of prophets—but the prophets are described as scribes, and they are clearly instructed in the law! In both chapters (5 and 23), however, we are to see Wisdom's envoys.

In Matt. 5:11–15 we recognize those whom Matthew regards as the *primary* audience of the Sermon. They are the scribes, the Salt and the Light of the world, to whom the true Torah is committed.

(3) In Matt. 5:16 we find the commission proper in the brief form: "Let your light so shine before men, that they may see your good works and give glory to your Father who is in heaven." At this point, it becomes apparent that Matthew has in view some group of opponents. Whether it is the Pharisaic scribes who "preach but do not practice" (23:3) or Christian false prophets who cry "Lord, Lord," but are evildoers (7:15–23) or both, is not for the moment of importance. In any case, the Christian scribe is told that unless he performs "good works" (I take it, follows the teaching) he has put his light under a bushel, made his salt insipid. The commission is, not merely to teach the law, but to do it to the glory of God.[58]

As envoys of Christ, the incarnate Wisdom, the disciples are charged with the responsibility of being good scribes—of "teaching the commandments," of "binding and loosing," of being "salt and light." This is not to say that the issuing of an eschatological proclamation or the preaching of the cross stands outside their range of duty as envoys of

---

56. But perhaps only because of our habits of thought, for Daniel is a wise man, Enoch and Ezra are scribes, etc. Apocalyptic is quite as much a product of the wisdom movement as of the prophetic (*cf.* G. von Rad, *Old Testament Theology*, 2: 301–315).

57. The beatitude concerning the "meek" has been interpolated.

58. The "city set on a hill" does not seem to belong here. However, the same association of metaphors is still found in the Gospel of Thomas, Sayings 32–33 (*cf.* Oxy. Pap. 1, lines 37–44).

Christ; the context of every commission makes this abundantly clear. On one side, however, they are representatives of the Torah, the appointed interpreters of the law, and in this function they are Wisdom's "prophets and wise men and scribes" (Matt. 23:34).

The Jesus who meets us in Q as σοφός and "child of Wisdom" brings truth to men; he is the mediator of divine revelation. The Jesus who meets us in Matthew retains his function as teacher and revealer, but he is no longer merely a prophet (albeit, the last and greatest) of Sophia. He *is* Wisdom and that means, as well, that he is the embodiment of Torah. Therefore,

Every one then who hears these words of mine and does them will be like a wise man who built his house upon the rock; and the rain fell, and the floods came, and the winds blew and beat upon the house, but it did not fall, because it had been founded on the rock (Matt. 7:24–25).

Epilogue

This study has been narrowly restricted in its aim and the reader may come to this point wondering if there ought not to have been another chapter—at least.

How is Matthew's understanding of Jesus as Wisdom incarnate to be integrated with the whole of his Christology, for example? It is perfectly clear that the Son of man concept is open to more extensive exploration from this perspective, and the argument of the last chapter—if it is correct—would appear to touch upon other messianic motifs, as well. Has not the investigation of Wisdom speculation in Matthew undertaken here led to other issues, barely touched upon but deserving of attention—like the relation of the evangelist's eschatology to the broader wisdom tradition, or the non-legal functions of the scribes of the Kingdom?

It must be admitted that the study leads up to some doors, opens them a crack, but does not cross their thresholds. To have explored such avenues further would have meant turning the enterprise in another direction and perhaps obscuring the basic exposition. Thus, the boundaries set at the outset have been adhered to, with the result that there is still work to be done.

Yet, I hope that the results of the study are such that its modest purposes have been achieved. My thesis was that Wisdom speculation was a major current in Matthew's Christian environment and that Matthew was a lively participant in the current. Although speculation about Sophia came to Matthew from at least one source, Q, in a form that was not wholly congenial to his understanding of Christ, he was not driven by that consideration to reject Wisdom thought. On the contrary, even his polemic tactic betrays his own allegiance to a similar tradition.

Matthew used the Wisdom themes in his own way. Whereas there were those by whom Jesus was viewed simply as the last in the long line of Wisdom's representatives, Matthew daringly identified Jesus with Wisdom. For the evangelist, Jesus was not Wisdom's child but Wisdom incarnate. Nor was Jesus only a prophet sent by Sophia; he was, instead, the Sender of prophets and wise men and scribes. In relation to the law, Jesus transcended familiar categories: as he was the incarnation of Wisdom, so was he the embodiment of Torah.

Therefore, Matthew's Jesus is fully entitled to issue the invitation: " Come to me, all who labor and are heavy-laden, and I will give you rest. Take my yoke upon you, and learn from me; for I am gentle and lowly in heart, and you will find rest for your souls. For my yoke is easy and my burden is light."

Index

131

Index

JUE